Empower Your Purpose: The Daniel FEAST

A Timeless Guide to Building Healthy Bodies and Relationships *Naturally!*

Empower Your Purpose: The Daniel FEAST

A Timeless Guide to Building Healthy Bodies and Relationships *Naturally!*

By Betsy Gwartney Catrett, N.D.

Tulsa, OK

DANIEL & company...*Naturally!* LLC
Copyright © 2003 by DANIEL & company...*Naturally!* LLC
Second Edition Copyright © 2009 by DANIEL & company...*Naturally!* LLC
Third Edition Copyright © 2014 by DANIEL & company...*Naturally!* LLC

Published by:
STORGOS PRESS
publisher@storgospress.com

Scriptures marked NIV are taken from the HOLY BIBLE, NEW INTERNATIONAL VERSION. Copyright © 1973, 1978, 1984 by International Bible Society. Used by permission of Zondervan Publishing House. All rights reserved.

Scriptures marked KJV are taken from the King James Version of the Bible.

Scriptures marked AMP are taken from THE AMPLIFIED BIBLE, Copyright © 1954, 1958, 1962, 1964, 1965, 1987 by The Lockman Foundation. All rights reserved. Used by permission (www.Lockman.org)

Scriptures marked MSG are taken from THE MESSAGE BIBLE. Copyright © 1993, 1994, 1995 by Eugene H. Peterson. All rights reserved. Used by permission of Tyndale House Publishers, Inc. Wheaton, Illinois. All rights reserved.

Scriptures marked TLB are taken from THE LIVING BIBLE, Copyright © 1971. Used by permission of Tyndale House Publishers, Inc. Wheat, Illinois. All rights reserved.

Scriptures marked NASB are taken from the NEW AMERICAN STANDARD BIBLE®, Copyright © 1960, 1962, 1963, 1968, 1971, 1972, 1973, 1975, 1977, 1995 by The Lockman Foundation. Used by permission.

Scriptures marked NLT are taken from the New Living Translation copyright © 1996, 2004, 2007 by Tyndale House Foundation. Used by permission of Tyndale House Publishers Inc., Carol Stream, Illinois 60188. All rights reserved. New Living, NLT, and the New Living Translation logo are registered trademarks of Tyndale House Publishers.

Scriptures marked CJB are taken from the Complete Jewish Bible by David H. Stern. Copyright © 1998. All rights reserved. Used by permission of Messianic Jewish Publishers, 6120 Day Long Lane, Clarksville, MD 21029. www.messianicjewish.net.

Scriptures marked NCV are taken from the New Century Version®. Copyright © 2005 by Thomas Nelson, Inc. Used by permission. All rights reserved.

Printed in the United States of America. All rights reserved.
No part of this publication may be reproduced in any form without the prior permission of the publisher. Contact information: betsy@danielandcompanynaturally.com

This book is for you if:

1. You feel dissatisfied and believe there has to be more to life than what you are experiencing.

2. You lack energy and just generally do not feel well; or you have aches and pains.

3. You are not sick or tired today, but you realize that you are living on caffeine and sugar; you know enough to wonder when your health is going to come crashing down … again?

4. Your children's behavior is a problem and you have "tried everything."

5. Your children are in one continual cycle of illness and/or allergies.

6. Deep rejuvenating sleep for those at your home is only a wish and a prayer.

7. You struggle with negativity and/or depression.

8. You feel irritable and frustrated much of the time.

9. Your family relationships are defined more by "co-existing" than a "family of friends".

10. Your relationships are falling apart.

ENDORSEMENTS:

"As a preventative medicine physician, I am delighted to give my endorsement to Dr. Catrett as she offers these resources. It is my hope that families will not only consider this program, but prioritize the time to shift their lifestyle into one that builds physical and relational health naturally. I agree with Betsy Gwartney Catrett that if these practices were implemented widely, we could see a decrease in disease, divorce, poverty, violence and crime."

Serena Tonstad, M.D., M.P.H., Ph.D. Professor
Health Promotion and Education School of Public
Health, Loma Linda University, Loma Linda, California

"This most refreshing undertaking is both practical and needed to give all who will participate, the motivation, encouragement and tools on how to find *lasting solutions* to those vital areas of life that we *all* struggle with: physical and relational health."

Joel Robbins, D.C., N.D.
Living Health Concepts, PLC

"I see the need for prevention and believe that the teaching through *The Daniel FEAST* can gently guide us to do just that. I also see why it's helpful and important to know what you are doing as you enter a Daniel Fast. Since the majority of our society lives on a junk food/fast food diet, a "cold turkey" departure can send them into serious withdrawal and detox. This would shift the focus from a spiritual nature to getting relief from the symptoms that are making them miserable, i.e. severe headaches, nausea, vomiting, aches, diarrhea, coughing, etc."

Daniel Ortega
Senior Minister
First Seventh Day Adventist Church
Tulsa, OK

"I am convinced that poor nutrition is a major factor in our mental and physical diseases; and that poverty, ignorance, and poor nutrition feed on one another and perpetuates the cycle."

Vickie Lee, DPh.
Retired Pharmacist
Hand-Up Minister

"Not only does she (Betsy Catrett) present knowledge, which leads to understanding, but she empowers and supports the reader through personal testimony and encouraging details. *Each chapter is carefully thought out with you, the reader, in mind. I can tell you that reading this book feels like sitting in her living room as she personally goes over each chart, dietary table, and worksheet.* As you read this book, decide for yourself. Are you going to follow the crowd and do what's always been done? You're sure to get the same results that millions of Americans are getting annually. Or you can decide to change your habits, and then change your life. You can be a healthier person, both physically and spiritually, and it can start today. I would encourage anyone wanting to make a lifestyle change to do the same as the prophet Daniel in the Old Testament: try it out and see if you're not healthier and happier. I'm sure you'll agree the results are undeniable."

Dr. Alex Himaya
Senior Pastor theChurch.at

"The information contained within Empower Your Purpose: The Daniel FEAST has the ability to not only improve your health, but possibly even save your life! Americans are among the sickest people on the planet. Mainstream medicine and the pharmaceutical industry have led most of us on a journey that will not and cannot sustain an optimal level of health. Why? Because the root cause of disease is never addressed. We cannot, by treating symptoms, ever achieve health. ... This book will provide you with the foundational information essential to achieving and maintaining health. Health, or the lack thereof, is determined by the hundreds of choices we make daily. These daily choices determine whether we will have a healthy body or a diseased body. *I encourage all readers to allow*

Betsy to lead you to wise choices that will empower your body to move toward the ultimate health God desires for each of us."

George Malkmus, Lit.D.
Founder Hallelujah Acres, Inc.

"I have always believed that those who are most effective in teaching a message are those who have been impacted by the message itself. Therefore, I would say that Betsy's diverse educational background coupled with her long-term, ongoing personal experience and effective, positive influence on those around her (which includes her immediate family of 21-14 grandchildren thus far- and an extended family of 55+), makes her exceptionally qualified to put together such practical curriculum. Aside from the evidentiary pages from various research projects that educate the reader, she presents us with practical, personally tested techniques, recipes and methods that are easy to follow for individuals and families alike. Every Christian home desiring to live life purposefully and healthy, according to God's will, should have a copy of this amazing book."

Daniel Ortega
Senior Minister
First Seventh Day Adventist Church
Tulsa, OK

"I am a junior in high school and play basketball on the varsity squad of a 6A school which has turned out state championship teams. This year Mrs. Gwartney had us try out the new plan. She told us to give her 10 days and tryout eating well. At first I was like…'Ah, I don't know.' But I gave it a shot, and after ten days I noticed how much my energy levels were increasing and how much better I felt when I was playing. And so now I've stuck with it until this very day, and it's been 3 months since basketball season was over."

A Junior in High School on a 6A
Basketball Team

"I just recently tried the (10 Day DANIEL lifestyle experience). At first I was a little bit iffy on it working out and everything. But it really turned out to be great. Some kids on our team only eat a bag of chewy candy before a game and they don't get much energy from that. But we got a whole lot of energy from all the whole grain bread and fresh produce we ate. It made us play a whole lot better. It was just a great experience."

A High School Freshman who lead his team to a 6A State Championship his Senior year.

"The teaching I received from DANIEL & company…Naturally!, has helped me stay healthy and physically fit during my time in the Marine Corps. My job is very demanding, both physically and mentally. Using these sound health principles, I have been able to prevent disease in my body and have passed on this information to the Marines under me."

Sargent in Unite States Marine Corps

"Juicing has been the *biggy* for me. I have gotten my cholesterol down to normal and off almost all of my medication. My energy is up and brain fog is down."

80 Year Old from Oklahoma

"Some things I learned from this course were #1,2,3 - how to eat, shop and cook healthy! Big "Aha." Healthy eating and preparation doesn't take that much more effort."

A Senior from Tulsa

"Thanks so much for the encouragement and comfort. I know that you don't have to be stuck in pain or disease. I've already seen so many wonderful changes from how I've changed my eating habits, my workout schedule, and my stress level. I so enjoy not having headaches every day like I used to - and not being able to go to the bathroom but 1-2 times a week. Plus, parts of my body have shaped up! I didn't even think I would notice a difference. It's been so cool. We could talk forever about this!"

An 18 year old from Georgia

Following are comments from students after a "growth group ladies' retreat" to learn and apply the teaching:

"This (teaching in a retreat setting) was wonderful! It was so helpful! I appreciate the practical help, as well as, the cooking suggestions and the Spiritual truths. Some things I learned in this course were #1 RAW. RAW. RAW! #2 Maximizing your energy by being selective of what you choose to put into your body. #3 There is a customized and gentle plan for your transition into this lifestyle. Have fun! Thank you for taking the time to teach us!"

JQ from Tulsa

"I learned about the design for our health, introduction to shopping wisely for foods that are good, better and best; and how to work towards that goal. This course gave me a path to begin on and help in getting there."

DC from Tulsa

"Some things I learned in this course were: #1 How important fresh and raw foods are in our diet. #2 Statistics of our nation's health. Suggestion I have to make this course better or more enjoyable in the future? It was wonderful! I can't think of anything to add. It's relevance to my life was in that I am a mother of two small children. I want to have us work toward optimal health. I would like more classes with Betsy!"

JW from Tulsa

"Some things I learned in this course were: #1 Meal and snack ideas. #2 How to acquire a taste - especially helpful with kids. *Relevance to*

my life: Made eating healthy look and taste good, as well as, showed how much eating healthy affects quality of life."

MB from Tulsa, OK

"Some things I learned in this course were: #1 How to make meals simpler and healthier. #2 How to organize my refrigerator. #3 How to make delicious juices and smoothies. *Relevance to me and my family:* I want to prevent further disease since we already have some. This retreat was understandable, enjoyable, clear, interesting, you were caring...perfect!

AZ from Tulsa, OK

"Some things I learned in this course: #1 Raw can be yummy. #2 Make this lifestyle change with grace. *Suggestions to make the course better or more enjoyable in the future?* No change needed – GREAT!"

MM from Tulsa, OK

"Some things I learned in this course were: #1 New, healthy cooking ideas, #2 Be humble with the new ideas (not everyone is ready for where you are in your journey), #3 This can be easy. Take it slow. *The relevance to my life:* It helped me to focus on what's important about my health. *Suggestions to make this course better or more enjoyable in the future?* It was perfect!"

AR from Broken Arrow, OK

"I so appreciate the message you are sending out with all your classes and love your gentle style of helping people to change old habits. If you ever need a new employee or want to open a much-needed Raw Food Restaurant in Tulsa...let me know! Thanks again!"

AR from Broken Arrow, OK (one year later)

DEDICATION

To my five sons, **Lars, Len, Lance, Lark and Luke:**
I'm so thankful to have been given the privilege of being your mother!
Each of you thrills my heart. Together we are discovering our
family's "assignment" and developing the potential
with which we were created.
It's fun to learn and grow together and to celebrate the hope we
have for building physical and relational health naturally. I love you
more than I have words to tell!

"No one who hopes in me ever regrets it." Isaiah 49 (MSG)

ACKNOWLEDGEMENTS

"Your body has many parts – limbs, organs, cells – but no matter how many parts you can name, you're still one body .... We each used to independently call our own shots, but then we entered into a large and integrated life in which He has the final say in everything .... I want you to think about how all this makes you more significant, not less. A body isn't just a single part blown up and into something huge.It's all the different-but-similar parts arranged and functioning together .... The way God designed our bodies is a model for understanding our lives together.Every part dependent on every other part, the parts we mention and the parts we don't. If one part hurts, every other part is involved in the hurt, and in the healing. If one part flourishes, every other part enters into the exuberance. You are Christ's body–that's who you are. You must never forget this. Only as you accept your part of that body does your "part" mean anything."
I Corinthians 12 (MSG)

It takes many parts to succeed in life. This work was originally produced during a very challenging season of my life, i.e., a ten-year season of single parenting five sons with very little resources of my own. Therefore, I needed a lot of people helping me/us. In the first edition, I listed the parts each one played. For this edition, I will only list the names. It is very difficult to recall every kindness and act of generosity that was received. I have done my best to recall the most significant ones here. Please forgive me if you were inadvertently left out.

Melba Demaree, Jeff and Barb Goss, Pat Bartlett, Joe Faulkner, Jeff and Nancie Brown, the Martin Blom Family, Esther Custer, Hope Center, East Tulsa Christian Church, Barbara Blachley, Joan Brown, Connie Butcher, Glenda Faulkner, Lyndia Grattopp, Marily Glass, Leigh Jacobs, Vickie Lee, Karen Robinson, Linda Taylor, Sherry LaBounty, Debra LaValleur, Laura Lindsey, Gayle Miller, Daphanie

Sholl, Salley Storey, Margaret Westphal, Catherine Zoller, Bob and Teresa Guillory, Curt and Becky Gwartney, Connie Maberry, Sarah LaBounty Loch, Mike (Migeli) Pantelogianis and Mark Whitney, the Perkins Families (Lloyd Perkins, Lincoln and Joan Brown, Gary and Janet Frakes), Dr. Joel Robbins, Leslie and Rob Robertson, David and Daphney Sholl, Ross and Linda Taylor, Sanctuary Fellowship of Christ Church, Russell and Margaret Westphal, David Wilson, Wright Christian Academy.

For this third edition, I would like to add Elizabeth Orellana, Rita Wisdom, and Becky Gwartney for the hours upon hours they invested to reformat this work and take it to a level I could not have achieved on my own. I would also like to add my precious husband, John Catrett, for his amazing spiritual and emotional support. A special thanks goes to Peter Biadasz and his marvelous team at Total Publishing & Media for the wonderful cover design and challenging layout (of this resource book with a plethora of design variety on nearly every page). Last but not least, a heartfelt thank you to Daniel J. Mawhinney, Darlene Shortridge, Jonna Feavel, and David Wilson for keeping hope alive when it looked like this work may end up on a back burner and not go forward at this time.

-Forever grateful, Betsy

TABLE OF CONTENTS

FOREWORD
Stamp of Approval xix

PREFACE
Who's Writing and Why xxiii

INTRODUCTION
Three Lifestyles Compared—Choose Life xxv

Lesson 1: REALITY
Experiments, Experiences and Statistics 1

Lesson 2: UNDERSTANDING
How It Happened—Blown Off Course 12

Lesson 3: SHIFTING
More Paradigms for Transitioning Back on Course 26

Lesson 4: HOW-TOs
The Set Up and the Process for the Daniel FEAST 50

Lesson 5: SYNERGY
Your Lifestyle on Course with Your Creator, Family and Friends 65

Lesson 6: GAME-ON
Four Levels of the DANIEL CHALLENGE 78

APPENDIX 1: Statistics 93
APPENDIX 2: Connecting Your Dots
(Identify YOUR Symptoms) 99
APPENDIX 3: How Food & Family
Have Changed Over Time 102
APPENDIX 4: Family Systems Evaluation 109
APPENDIX 5: Peter's Vision (Scriptures) 110

APPENDIX 6:	DANIEL CHALLENGE Replacement Plan & Journal	112
APPENDIX 7:	Budget Worksheet	117
APPENDIX 8:	Cravings	119
APPENDIX 9:	Guide to Soaking Nuts and Seeds	122
APPENDIX 10:	Additional Tips for Finicky or Reluctant Eaters	123
APPENDIX 11:	The Dirty Dozen and Clean Fifteen of Produce	128
APPENDIX 12:	Miracle in Wisconsin	131
APPENDIX 13:	Prayers for Being Born Again & God's Help as Your Creator	134
APPENDIX 14:	Scriptures for Reference and Memorization	136
APPENDIX 15:	Paradigm Shifts and Connect the Dots Statements	144
APPENDIX 16:	Talking to Your Health Care Provider	149
TOPICAL INDEX BY CHAPTER		150
DISCUSSION QUESTIONS		155

FOREWORD

Stamp of Approval

Many churches across America are calling for DANIEL FASTS these days. The reasons for this may vary greatly. Some desire a deeper walk with the Lord and use the Daniel Fast (in a way that feels sacrificial to their present lifestyle) as a means to accomplish this. Some churches are seeking answers to problems or new direction and want to heighten their spiritual experience. Others have, in their church's roots, the understanding of the importance of knowing and walking in their Creator's design for health, but over the years have not put as strong an emphasis on it as they once did, thus the Daniel Fast refocus.

I have observed over the last decade that most everyone is slowly starting to realize the enormity of our nation's health problem, and they are beginning to look for solutions that transcend the limitations of our typical symptom-covering-pills-and-surgery options. People are starting to recognize and admit that there *are* natural, yet effective, solutions. And as evidence has shown, the Daniel Fast or Lifestyle solves our health problems at the very core.

As for *our* church, from our denomination's foundation we've recognized that the DANIEL FAST faithfully and effectively accomplishes multiple things that can be summarized in the following way: The first and most obvious is the physical freedom from pain and discomforts. It can be surprising to some to see the positive changes that this FAST can produce physically and psychologically in such a short period of time. Second, they will experience an increase of energy for creativity and planning. Those whose lives involve quick and fast paced thinking will reap the benefits in their ability to better and more quickly process information. And as a pastor I cannot go on without emphasizing the clarity of thought one receives when it comes to spiritual discernment. And last but not least, I believe that we fall in line to follow God's will for our lives when we are living a healthy lifestyle; a plan where God desires for us to prosper, to have a future and hope.

I understand that Betsy Catrett, N.D. is coming from a naturopathic perspective, which includes a holistic approach to living, looking at the whole person—spiritual, relational, purpose in life, exercise, etc. and not just diet. So, her desire would be that those of us calling for a Daniel *Fast*, following the Biblical Daniel's *Diet*, would also encourage our congregations to move into a Daniel *Lifestyle* with many wonderful health-building components, and accept the *DANIEL CHALLENGE* to fully apply this to our lives. This would enable us to see for ourselves what the counter culture of Daniel's day also saw as a result of the 10-day test.

What we see from this teaching is that a "fast" from the Standard American Diet (S.A.D.!) of stimulation (through caffeine, sugar, processed, chemically laden foods) while adding back the fruits, veggies, nuts, whole grains, seeds, legumes, and purified water is not really a fast at all, but rather the FEAST that a generous and loving Creator lavished upon us.

As a minister with a responsibility to visit the sick and officiate funerals for the dead, I have an ongoing fresh "revelation" on the great need for this teaching. Not only do the sick miss out on ministry opportunities, but their caregivers do, too. As a matter of fact, the prayer lists of most churches are consumed with requests for health related issues rather than concerns for the souls of the lost, spiritual growth, and practical needs.

I see the need for prevention and believe that the teaching through *Empower Your Purpose: The Daniel FEAST!* can gently guide us to do just that. I also see why it's helpful and important to know what you are doing as you enter a Daniel Fast. Since the majority of our society lives on a junk food/fast food diet, a "cold turkey" departure can send them into serious withdrawal and detox. This would shift the focus from a spiritual nature to getting relief from the symptoms that are making them miserable, i.e., severe headaches, nausea, vomiting, ache, diarrhea, coughing, etc.

As one born into the Seventh-day Adventist denomination where a focus on health is definitely part of the D.N.A. of the church, I have heard various health messages my *entire* life. During my ministry I have worked with many wonderful men and woman dedicated to teaching biblical, yet practical ways to bring true health back to people's lives. I believe it's important to offer effective teaching from a variety of perspectives. **This work by Betsy Catrett clearly centers on Biblical teaching and *is the best I have ever seen*, in that it is so non-condemning and do-able.** I have always believed that those who are most effective in teaching a message are those who have been impacted by the message itself. Therefore I would say that Betsy's diverse educational background coupled with her long-term, ongoing personal experience and effective, positive influence on those around her (which includes her immediate family of 21–14 grandchildren thus far–and an extended family of 55+), makes her exceptionally qualified to put together such practical curriculum. Aside from the evidentiary pages from various research projects that educate the reader, she presents us with practical, personally tested techniques, recipes and methods that are easy to follow for individuals and families alike.

Every Christian home desiring to live life purposefully and healthy according to God's will should have a copy of this amazing book. It will have an ever-present effect on the lives of those who take pleasure in its guidance and instruction. I highly endorse this work as a non-condemning, do-able and fun short course with a time-tested, historic role model.

Daniel Ortega, Senior Pastor First Seventh Day Adventist Church, Tulsa, OK

"Beloved, I pray that you may prosper in all things and be in health, just as your soul prospers" 3 John 1:2

PREFACE

More often than not, life doesn't play fair. You start out with something that seems very beautiful and that fills you with hope, but then you find yourself turned upside down, dangling precariously and painfully by one toe, then dropped on your head without so much as an, "I'm sorry!"

Can any of you relate to that? I can. *The Reader's Digest* version of my story goes something like this. I married my sixth-grade sweetheart. We had five wonderful sons together. How could life be richer, right? So it seemed. But underneath the beauty were some dangerous beliefs that would sabotage our dreams. (Don't be fooled. What you DON'T KNOW can KILL YOU! And what you *do* know and *don't apply* can too!) Here's how it played out in my life: My father died prematurely on the operating table with a heart valve replacement, and I found myself in a situation with my husband where I felt the need to ask him for a legal separation so we could push a "reset button" on our marriage. Problem was, against my beliefs and desires, divorce took place instead. Ouch! My two most significant male relationships were gone through disease and divorce. Ouch Ouch! I had less than one dollar to my name, an incomplete education, and five sons to steer to maturity. Ouch Ouch Ouch Ouch OUCH!!!!!

When things like this happen, we can become bitter, or we can become better. We can become sour or make lemonade, right? Oh sure! We have all heard these cliques, but it did not look hopeful at the time. Prayer. Trust. Soon educational doors began to open for me. One opportunity followed another. We were on our way. I was learning how to reverse the downward spiral our lives were taking in order to become the *transitional generation* in some specific areas. It was <u>exciting</u> to know that our choices would increase the possibilities that the next generation wouldn't have to go through all this heartache.

I obtained an undergraduate multidisciplinary degree in Psychology, Sociology, Communications and Geriatrics, a license to administrate

Residential Care facilities in the state of Oklahoma, and then went on to get two more degrees as a Natural Health Consultant and a Naturopathic Doctor. This increased my hope for healthy family relationships and healthy bodies. Dr. Ruby Payne's *Train the Trainers Certification* in "Framework for Understanding Poverty" interested me, as well as her work on "Bridges Out of Poverty," so I certified in both programs, receiving additional tools and insights for helping others overcome the poverty that oftentimes comes out of disease and divorce (generational poverty, too). Prepare and Enrich Marriage Counseling and P.L.A.C.E. Counseling Certification gave me tools to help myself and others more fully celebrate our personal designs and diversity, plus much more insight, understanding and tools to create happy marriages. I worked for a season in Permanency Planning and Foster Care for Oklahoma Department of Human Services Child Welfare Division and mediating for the Supreme Court of Oklahoma in Civil, Family and Divorce, as well as Child Welfare cases. These experiences have brought me full circle from being *IN* the system to helping others get *OUT* of the system.

I hope this helps you recognize my motives and passion for this work. Thank God that not everyone will experience the devastations we did. Currently, many are experiencing this devastation and your system of family and friends may be a part of these statistics.

There are many components to building health and happiness. In this book, we have expounded upon the dietary component and provided thoughts to guide you into the purpose, identity, and relational components, which yield successful living. The opening stories in each chapter have come out of these life experiences and I trust will give you an understanding of what we are dealing with in our culture. I believe that the materials following those stories will increase your confidence so that you and your family don't have to experience much of the pain and loss we have, but rather feel empowered to fulfill the purpose for which you were created. God bless you as you take a look at these exciting truths.

INTRODUCTION

Three Lifestyles Compared—Choose Life

#1 ILLEGAL DRUG LIFESTYLE - I clung to the door handle of Andy's S.U.V. as we worked our way through the chuckholes of the driveway in this rural setting. Before me were two mobile homes, one to my left and one to my right. We wound our way through the maze of broken-down cars, sun-faded toys, and over-grown grass to the front door of the left mobile home, the place our report described as the investigation site. At the sound of our knock, an elderly woman opened the door, letting a flood of cigarette smoke mixed with the distinct aroma of stale frying grease escape into our faces. We introduced ourselves to the apparent matriarch of this family and inquired about the people we were there to see. There had been a report of child abuse/neglect at this resident.

After the initial dialogue, we discovered that the parents of the alleged abused children were not there, hadn't been there in days, and the elderly lady claimed that she didn't know where they were. So, she proceeded to take us to the mobile home next door. We could smell the contents of the home long before reaching the top step of the porch. Flies swarmed around the front door.

"Watch your step, Betsy," Andy said as we moved through the door, which had a gaping hole in the lower part about the size of a man's boot, then stepped over broken glass and animal feces into the front room.

It was hard to concentrate with that awful stench permeating the room. Soiled diapers were left to lie around from some child who was probably laid on the dirty, ragged carpet or on top of the dirty clothes that were strewn around the room. Animal feces were everywhere, and urine stains were obvious where the carpet had been used as a litter pan. The kitchen counter tops and dining table were completely covered with dirty dishes, leftover food, dirty pots, fast food containers, and an enormous number of flies! Windows were broken out, toilets not flushed, and the house was obviously void of any type of cleaning for quite some time, which was apparent when we saw the layers of filth encrusted on everything.

When we were alone, Andy said, "Welcome to Department of Human Services Investigative Unit." (Andy was training me, as I was new on the job.) "This is what the home of a meth user typically looks like," he went on to say. "Can you imagine babies, toddlers, and children living here? These people typically start their day with a fix, like others start with coffee, and the day goes downhill from there. They need so much help to be free to become all they were designed to be and to carry the responsibility they have for their children–never mind attempting to be contributors in the community."

It was *easy* for me to see the need for change here.

Meth **promised:**	Meth **delivered:**
* Fun and a feel-good experience	* Pain, heartache, suffering, misery, withdrawal, and heartache from loss of health, function, dignity, and early death
* Freedom from the pain of life	* More pain/problems than before drugs as there was "never enough money," eviction, law enforcement, and breakup of the family were typically part of the scenario
* A place to belong with other users	* Loneliness when "friends" take advantage of or even abandon

#2 BLUE ZONE LIFESTYLE - Fast forward three years later. I was at home in my downtown Tulsa high-rise condominium when the phone rang. It was my friend, Joan. "Betsy, are you at home right now?"

"Yes," I replied, "just walked in the door."

"Well, turn on Oprah right quick. There's someone on there with her and Dr. Oz that I think you will want to see."

So, I did as she suggested and sure enough, there was Dr. Oz and Oprah interviewing a man named Dan Buettner. They introduced Mr. Buettner as author of *The Blue Zones*, a book that chronicles the commission from *National Geographic* for him and his team to locate the largest populations of 100-year-old people worldwide. They found four areas with significant numbers of 100-year-old (and older) people living without disease.

The first community they found was in Sardinia, Italy, where they looked over the waters and dubbed it a "blue zone." This name stuck for the project. They also found large groups in Okinawa, Japan; Loma Linda, California; and Nicoya Peninsula in Costa Rica.

I hopped on a plane and went to see for myself in Loma Linda, California. I went to the very places where Dr. Oz interviewed people who were experiencing life into triple digits with virtually no disease. Their minds were sharp, and they were still able to make contributions into the lives of others. For example, in 2005, Seventh-day Adventist Marge Jetton (who signed my copy of *National Geographic* with her picture in it) renewed her driver's license after turning 100 years old. She lives alone, fills her own car with gas, exercises at the gym and volunteers in many venues each week! (http://travel.nationalgeographic.com/travel/happiest-places/blue-zones/ http://www.bluezones.com/wp-content/uploads/2011/02/Nat_Geo_Longevity.pdf) These centenarians are experiencing life at its best. Through the interviews, I learned that:

Life in the Blue Zones of holistic, **promised:**	Life in the Blue Zones of holistic, healthy, living healthy, living **delivered:**
* Satisfaction in life and positive experiences	* Satisfaction in life and positive experiences
*Dignity and respect	* Dignity and respect
* A place to belong with people they loved	* A place to belong with people they loved
* Clear thinking	* Clear thinking
* Freedom from physical pain	* Freedom from physical pain
* Energy for creativity and planning	* Energy for creativity and planning
* A meaningful and purposeful existence (responsibly with one's own family and in the bigger picture of community)	* A meaningful and purposeful existence (responsibly with one's own family and in the bigger picture of community)

The lifestyles we just described are examples of two opposites within our society. One is blatantly in need of change; and one is quite some distance from the typical American lifestyle, otherwise known as "Standard American Diet/Lifestyle (S.A.D.)."

#3 STANDARD AMERICAN DIET (S.A.D.) LIFESTYLE - So, "What exactly is the **S**tandard **A**merican **D**iet/Lifestyle?" you may ask. I'll bet you already know what it is. If you are the typical American, you hear the alarm clock go off in the morning, punch the snooze button three times because your body aches and your energy is so low that you are having difficulty getting out of bed. But alas, you stumble to the coffee pot, pour a super-size to-go cup full and add spoons of sugar to the specialty coffee that was set to brew the night before. Because you overslept and had to locate Susie's homework (the dog pointed it out under the pillow on the couch with a white bread bologna sandwich on top of it), there was no time for the usual Captain Terrific Super Duper Crunchy cereal and milk. Neither was there time to make the regular "healthy" lunchable with "fruit" rollups and sugar-laden granola bars for lunches. The madness of carpooling and rush hour traffic on the way to drop off kids and get to work on time had begun.

So you cruise through the closest drive-thru or whip into the nearest Quickie Mart to pick up more stimulation in the form of glazed donuts or some other unhealthy "breakfast" food. Oh, and don't forget the energy drink filled with enough caffeine to kill a small animal for the afternoon lag. You give the kids money for the pizza, cheese sticks and dessert served in the cafeteria. So, the every-two-hour-stimulant-to-get-me-through-the-day period has begun. It comes in the form of caffeine, sugar, salt, and processed foods.

You eat your lunch at your desk, trying not to crunch in the ear of your client on the other end of the phone. *Now where were those antacids? I'd almost take up smoking just to have a break from the office! I'd really rather take a nap, however!*

The workday is over and the parenting day is just gearing up. *No groceries at home. Ugh! What to fix the kids for dinner? Dinner? No time for dinner. Tonight is cheer practice, drama club and a soccer game. Oh, WHY did we let them all sign up for activities in the same semester? Oh well, it is what it is. Drive-thru again. Burgers, fries, shakes...before a game? Ok, tacos then! At least it has lettuce in it.* "Carry Out" bags are passed all the way to the back of the SUV. "And you'd better not be hyper after drinking that Route 44 cherry lime-aid. DO YOU HEAR ME?! Don't talk. You've got 5 minutes before we get there. Eat!"

It's now 9:30. Everyone has been picked up from the evening activities and you are heading home to shower and bed. *Oh no...<u>homework</u> and...the SCIENCE FAIR tomorrow? I thought that was NEXT week.* After scrambling for over an hour to slap together Popsicle sticks in a trapezoidal formation for the science project, all the kids are finally in bed. You drag yourself to your room and put on PJ's, promising to brush your teeth twice the next day. You set the alarm clock for the next morning. It seems that no sooner than your head hits the pillow, it goes off, and the crazy cycle starts all over again.

> It's reported that $.91 out of every dollar is spent on processed foods that do not qualify as health building, energizing food/fuel for the body. In other words, only $.09 out of every American dollar is spent on "food" used for "body fuel" that gives life. It is also reported that the average American youth will go up to two weeks without consuming anything *living*. Unbelievable!

The typical American lifestyle **promised:**	The typical American lifestyle **delivered:**
* Speed, convenience, and ease	* A slowed down lifestyle with inconvenient illnesses, difficulty getting off work or out of school, etc. to get to doctor appointments and the pharmacy.
* Cheap meals	* Financial pressures to pay the monthly health insurance premium (because you just CAN'T do without it) or cost of doctor's appointments, specialist appointments, prescription and over-the-counter drugs, extra trips to the dentists for the cavities, etc. (The number one

	cause of bankruptcy in America is medical debt. The number two cause of divorce is financial stress.)
* Temporary pleasurable escape from life's pain and exhaustion when you began to eat these "fast foods"	* More pain and problems than you had before you used food to comfort, anesthetize or stimulate
* A connection: "Everybody's doing it" "I can do what I want!"	* A connection: Medically! where you aren't in control because you're too ill and others are caring for you
* Fun. Fun. Belonging to the "Pig Out Club"	* Excessive weight and many of the painful ailments that accompany it.
* A comforting "familiar"	* Fear of the unknown when you are in an unfamiliar medical arena

It is easy for us to call the "meth lifestyle" harmful to people as well as to society. The consequences of that lifestyle are obviously destructive. However, it's not as easy to see how damaging the typical American lifestyle is until you take a step back and look at the negative results of this lifestyle that society has come to accept as "normal".

Just because something is "normal" for a group of people doesn't mean it's healthy or "good." It's normal for drug addicts to start their day off with a "fix" but that doesn't make it good. It's "normal" for most Americans to suffer frequent illness, allergies, lack of energy, and it's normal for them to deal with their disease symptoms by making trips to the doctor and taking numerous over-the-counter and prescription drugs… but that doesn't mean it's healthy or that it's the way it 'has to be'. There is a better way.

Both of these lifestyles have a common issue at their core. They both want to experience something better but lack either the knowledge or the understanding of how to make the transition. The common goal is a lifestyle that produces the good results, which everyone wants, without all of the negative side effects.

There are millions of people in America today who have no clue that even in this day and age we really can live past the century mark and still live productive, pleasant and disease-free lives.

Others may have knowledge and understanding, but what they lack is empowerment through God's word and the support of others to help them to make positive lifestyle choices. They know what steps to take but end up not following through, leaving them feeling guilt-ridden, hungry and frustrated.

We were created for more than a lifestyle of pain, stress, illness and fatigue. I believe we were designed with a greater purpose, one that doesn't include struggling with "senior moments" in our middle age and living with chronic degenerative disease that can plague us for 20 years or more before death. Americans are dying too long and living too short. Let's not just settle for quantity of life, but QUALITY of life as well!

Research has proven that we *can* enjoy an energetic, vibrant, abundant, and disease-free life up until we breathe our final breath. And right now, there are a myriad of people all over the world who are doing just that.

I have seen these centenarians with my own eyes! I've watched people with cancer, gangrene, hypertension, diabetes, etc, restored to perfect health. Not only have I seen others recover, but by following some simple steps I have experienced health rejuvenation for myself. In just 100 short days I saw all my symptoms, such as shortness of breath, brain fog, achy joints, insomnia, and heart palpitations, disappear. I lost over 20 pounds, increased my jogging from 3 miles (it took me five years to build up to that) to running a half-marathon distance of 13.1 miles; AND all this happened after I turned 50 years old!

> Americans are dying too long and living too short. Let's not just settle for quantity of life, but QUALITY of life as well!

Experiencing a lifestyle like this for yourself may seem difficult or even impossible, but I know from firsthand experience that it is achievable if you have someone to show you the steps to take.

We are made for this kind of healthy living. You are worth it! You have value! You are needed to make a healthy, functional, powerful society! You matter! Life can be unbelievably wonderful! Life doesn't have to be filled with physical pain and discomfort as the result of illness and disease. It can truly be like heaven on earth!

Dedicate yourself to fully and consistently learn and apply the teaching. Become lifelong seekers of truth - to customize to your situation. Enjoy the benefits. Make no mistake; progress can be made when any amount of truth is applied.

This book will show you the simple, easy, non-condemning and non-judgmental step-by-step actions you can take today so that you can transition from the lifestyle that doesn't deliver what it promises into one that delivers everything it promises and more! And you can get started right now!

In this book you will be given assistance to connect the dots that create a health building *lifestyle*. You will also be introduced to a role model named Daniel whose wise application of these health-building  principles and paradigm shifts gave him health, vigor and vitality that each of us can experience. (Watch for these graphics throughout the book, which will emphasize the **connect the dots** and **paradigm shift** statements.)

Now let's begin this journey with a more in-depth look at the typical American lifestyle, the consequences that it is currently generating, and see if we can find exactly where we got off track.

Class Preparation: Read through the stats in Appendix 1. Take a few minutes to make note of which ones stand out most to you and which ones you see that have affected your life (or your family's lives) the most.

*" ... test us ... see how we look compared to the other young men who are eating the king's food.
Then make your decision in light of what you see."*

Lesson 1 – REALITY

Experiments, Experiences and Statistics

Picnic basket? Check. Water cooler? Check. Blanket? Check. Diaper bag with extra diapers and changes of clothes? Check. Things to do in the car? Check. "Okay everyone get in the car," I called to the boys out the back porch door. Off the slide, the Jungle Jim, the 3-story tree house, and across the bridge over the wet-weather creek they came running. We were going on a family outing to a small town in northeastern Oklahoma. The boys' daddy had a business responsibility to care for and we were combining business with pleasure. It was a warm summer day with the promise of a scorcher by noon. No worries; we'd be back in plenty of time to head to the spring-fed creek to cool off. What a fun day we had planned! But that's not exactly how it played out. The boys got busy on their in-the-car-on-longer-trips activities and the time passed quickly. Before we knew it we were in the foothills of the Ozarks, going up and down steeper inclines, when I heard my husband say, "Uh oh!"

"What's wrong?" I responded.

"The temperature light just came on and the temperature gauge is rising rapidly. Should we try to make it to town?" (You say things like this when you are inexperienced!) Ignoring the warning light, we continued on. Before long, steam was coming out of the sides of the hood. We pulled over on the side of the road and lifted the hood. Steam was spewing out of the radiator. No problem; we had a water cooler full of ice cold water that would help cool it down in no time. (I can just hear some of you now shouting, "Nooooo!") For those of you who

have never had a problem like this, let me just say that the gauges were not the problem. **It didn't help the situation to ignore the warning lights.** *(The warning lights were just symptoms of the root problem.) It wouldn't have helped the situation if we had put a bandage over those lights. It didn't help to do the wrong thing to try to fix the problem. The day didn't end as planned. No one enjoyed a cool swim in the creek, and there was no income from a potential business opportunity. Instead, the outcome was the loss of a vehicle because of a cracked head, seven very hot, tired, and grumpy family members, a hitchhike ride home, and life lessons waiting to be discovered.*

What did we need to learn? What many of you are probably beginning to learn: That the unhealthy lifestyles that plague our nation are affecting more than our pocketbooks and budgets; they are affecting our very lives. The warning lights are flashing – fatigue, sleeplessness, irritability, weight gain, disease, etc. – and the problem needs to be addressed before it ruins more than a family outing. So, what can be done about it?

First, let's explore the possibility of a **paradigm shift**. We have always felt that symptoms were "the enemy," or the problem, haven't we? You must stop a runny nose or a cough because they are inconvenient and troublesome. You must anesthetize any pain so that you may continue on with your day. But what if that perspective isn't solving your health crisis?

When you are in your vehicle, do you pay attention to the gas gauge or warning lights that may appear on your dash? What are they telling you? What information do they pass along to the occupants? If the gas gauge displays an "E," it's time to stop and get fuel. If a warning light comes on, someone better check the owner's manual. These signs point to a problem, and it needs to be resolved. Will you unplug the alarm or the warning light so the noise or light won't bother you? Will you ignore it and risk destruction – not only for you, but also for your passengers?

Now imagine that the warning light on your dash, or the "E" showing on your gas gauge, is a physical symptom. If there is pain in your leg while playing soccer, rather than ignore the "empty fuel gauge" why not assess what is wrong? I know of a young man who played a game with a broken femur while taking pain pills! In that weakened state, the bone could have broken completely and perforated the skin. Likewise, a diabetic who ignores blood sugar symptoms, and continues to fuel the body with sugars, may suffer the consequences of blindness and/or amputation of their feet. Do you want a temporary solution to silence the symptom, possibly resulting in a potentially large and complex problem? Or, do you want to learn the skills and assume responsibility for the things you have done to cause the problems and begin to build your health?

> Stopping the symptoms doesn't eliminate disease any more than covering the temperature gauge of the car prevents a cracked block.

Therefore, the **paradigm shift** that needs to be made would be as follows: Rather than focusing on the symptoms being the problem, focus on a violation of human design and a culture full of toxicity as being the problem. Define symptoms as our friends to reveal what nutrients are low in our body and thus, what foods need to be added to our diet. Giving the body time to deal with the symptoms may take a little bit longer in the present, but may save you from facing surgery or years of disease later. Personal responsibility for adjusting one's lifestyle would be taken, and the fight to stop the symptoms would end. Whoa, now that's different!

Health care practitioners are dedicated to relieving your pain and suffering. Many of them know that lack of exercise, fresh air, sunshine, purpose, strong relationships and healthy food results in poor health; but their patient/consumer comes to them wanting a quick fix and expects to leave with a pill or a promise of surgery to fix the pain. When enough of their patients hold to this demand, they stop trying to make suggestions of health-building options. (Some of them never even attempt anything but the drugs and surgery route.) NOTE: For further study read *Dead Doctors Don't Lie* by Dr. Joel Wallach, Wellness Publications.

To makes things worse, just listen to the TV commercials during the evening news, and you will notice all of the ads for drugs that promise to alleviate certain symptoms (along with 10 to 20 plus potential side affects)! We must ask ourselves, "Are we juggling symptoms or taking responsibility for building our health?" **Is this getting to the root of our symptoms or compounding our problem?**

The Pottinger Experiment

In the 1940's, a medical doctor, Francis M. Pottinger, funded his own research and prepared an experiment using 900 cats to determine what effects processed food had on the body. The cats were divided into five groups. Two of the groups were fed whole foods (*raw* milk and meat) that were **natural foods** for cats. The other three groups were given **denatured foods** that were unlike the food cats eat naturally (pasteurized, evaporated, and condensed milk). All of the groups were fed the same minimal basic diet to sustain life. However, the predominant portions of the diets were either real foods or denatured foods as listed above. The cats were observed over a four-generational period and Dr. Pottinger documented the following results:

Group:	A	B	C	D	E
Diet Fed	Raw meat	Raw milk	Pasteurized milk	Evaporated milk	Condensed milk
1st Generation	Remained healthy		Developed disease and illness **near end of life.**		
2nd Generation	Remained healthy		Developed disease and illness **mid life.**		
3rd Generation	Remained healthy		Developed disease and illness in the **beginning of life.** Many died before 6 months of age.		
4th Generation	Remained healthy		**No fourth generation was produced.** Either 3rd generation parents were sterile, or the offspring were naturally aborted.		

Look at the progression of "cause and effect/sowing and reaping" from generation to generation among the animals fed a **denatured diet** in which important enzymes are killed through heat preparation. It would be similar to our modern junk food. Are we not experiencing much the same results in humans today? Are you aware of children with juvenile diabetes, arthritis, and heart disease, etc. - diseases that were once only seen in old age? My daughter-in-law's high-risk pregnancy specialist told her that 50% of today's young women are unable to conceive, and miscarriages are at an all-time high. It has now been four generations since 1900. Pottinger's experiment is ringing true for humans, too.

It's interesting that people with an investment in show animals or horticulture fully understand the importance of feeding their animals (and plants) a **natural diet** that achieves health, strength, beauty and reproduction. Why do **humans** think that dead food produces life-giving, strong, beautiful bodies?

> "Are we juggling symptoms or taking responsibility for building our health?" Is this getting to the root of our symptoms or compounding our problem?

My husband and I are connected to several wonderful health building groups. We are all seeing firsthand the reversal of disease, infertility, and the healing of long endured injuries. There *is* hope for so many who feel hopeless.

Senior Care Experiences

I worked approximately 2,000 hours in the senior care unit of a hospital. My responsibilities in case management included taking a Bio-Psycho-Social Summary and Assessment of each patient. I had to interview the patient and/or the patient's family to gain information concerning their biological, psychological, and social history and how that—contributed to their admission to the psychiatric unit of the hospital. What was most interesting was the predictability of certain conditions, both physical and relational, resulting from certain decisions or circumstances in one's life. Needless to say, we reap what we sow; unfortunately, we often reap what others sow as well. Exploring the lifestyles of our family and other support systems is very important. However, it is also important to note that many symptoms are not as much genetic as they are diet and lifestyle related.

Many of the patients were admitted with symptoms of dementia. They were oftentimes given a drug holiday–taking the patient off all drugs and adding them back one at a time to see which ones were still needed and causing the brain function problem. Another treatment was to clean out their colon. The patients were so constipated that the toxins in their bowels were just recirculating and causing loss of mental function. When they were cleaned out, they functioned much better. We know how much our seniors are vital to our own lives and to our families and our communities. When filled with toxins, though, the vitality of their lives and their contribution to life is diminished greatly.

During my undergraduate studies, I was first introduced to the term "Granny Dumping". I couldn't imagine that there were places in this country where it was common for the family of an elderly person to drop them off at a hospital and never return. The responsibility of caring for a demented, uncooperative, and financially destitute person was just too overwhelming. That's a far cry from the Blue Zone example we learned about (in the Introduction) where seniors are healthy, functioning, loving, and contributing to large family systems and the community until death at the century mark!!!

> We are all seeing firsthand the reversal of disease, infertility, and the healing of long endured injuries. There *is* hope for so many who feel hopeless.

Consider this:
How do you want to live in your senior years?

WITH ILLNESS	WITH HEALTH
Pain (relational and physical)	Passions and Opportunities (free from pain) Pleasure of Vitality
Loss of activities and independence	Choice of activities and enjoyment of independence (mobility and energy)
Doctor and pharmacies dictating how you spend your time and resources	Using your time and resources to fulfill you purpose and contribute to other's successes
Managed care dictating course of treatment	Your own resources to build health naturally and enjoy the process

Think about it: Are we building health or merely juggling symptoms? Juggling symptoms does not constitute health. A body without disease and full of vibrant energy does. Just because something is common doesn't mean that it's normal. Is it really necessary to have so many health issues as we age? This accepted theory is disproved in our modern day Blue Zone study.

A holistic approach to building health includes one's spirituality.

"In the beginning God created ..."
Genesis 1:1 (NIV)

"So God created man in his own image ..."
Genesis 1:27 (NIV)

"For I know the plans I have for you," declares the Lord, "plans to prosper you and not to harm you, plans to give you hope and a future."
Jeremiah 29:11(NIV)

"Thou wilt show me the path of life: in Thy presence is fullness of joy; at Thy right hand there are pleasures for evermore."
Psalm 16:11(KJV)

"Thou art worthy, O Lord, to receive glory and honour and power: for thou hast created all things, & for thy pleasure they are and were created."
Revelation 4:11(KJV)

"The thief comes only to steal and kill and destroy; I came that they may have life, and have it abundantly."
John 10:10 (NASB)

When we know God as our Creator, understand and follow His design for our relationships and the care of our body (His temple), we will break the cycle of destructive lifestyle patterns and behaviors of our biological family systems and begin to see God's blessings flow from ourselves to our children, grandchildren, great grandchildren.

*"The Lord is slow to anger, abounding in love and forgiving sin and rebellion. Yet He does not leave the guilty unpunished; He punishes the children for the sin of the fathers to the **third and fourth generation**."*
Numbers 14:18 (NIV, emphasis mine)

*"...but showing love to a **thousand generations** of those who love Me and <u>keep My commandments</u>."*
Deuteronomy 5:10 (NIV, emphasis mine)

These scriptures show that there are generational patterns of behavior and the consequences that result from the behaviors. Lest there be some precious souls taking this course who are suffering from debilitating circumstances that are not associated with generational choices, let me hasten to say that John 9:3 validates that possibility. We don't want those whose malady was designed directly for the purpose of glorifying God to be confused with consequences. I would venture to say that there are far more of us who suffer with the consequences of choices (generational and our own). Therefore, it is wise for us to explore the possibility that we are to be the transitional generation to move from health-robbing behaviors to ones that build health.

About this time in a lesson on building health, two big demons try to take over. Let's not let them.

The Demons of Guilt and Condemnation

It is of the utmost importance that we set the stage for our health-building study with a *positive* focus, a focus that will free us to learn and grow. We need to avoid wasting valuable time and energy beating ourselves up over "failures" that we experience as individuals, families and nations. For example, let's say a cruise ship was sailing from New York to London. In the course of the trip it encounters unusually strong currents followed by a horrific storm. Would anyone **condemn** the captain for getting off course?

Of course not! This is a **normal occurrence** for such a challenging trip. The ship's captain will simply make adjustments to get back onto the right course. It might take longer to get to the destination, but they will get there! Spectators will cheer for the ship's passengers and crew as they arrive because the captain acknowledged that they were off course, overcame the difficulties, and then got back on the right course with a strong finish.

> *"Therefore, there is now no condemnation for those who are in Christ Jesus."*
> Romans 8:1(NIV)

We must focus on maturing to the point that we understand cause and effect; we must **connect the dots** and see where we are going with our choices in the long run instead of doing what feels good now for the short run. We make better choices as a result of our understanding. We must care about how our choices affect others in the bigger picture of community and life.

If you need a little more help to **connect *your* dots**, consider completing the *Connecting Your Dots* charts in Appendix 2. (This has been adapted from The Hallelujah Diet by George Malkmus with Peter & Stowe Shockey.) It will help you see where your present choices have taken you and will continue to take you, where your new choices will take you and will continue to take you, and give you tools that will help you make the transition.

"You are living a brand new kind of life that is continually learning more and more of what is right..."
Colossians 3:10 (TLB)

> We must care about how our choices affect others in the bigger picture of community and life.

It's obvious that many of us have gone off course and we must do something to make it right. A **transitional generation** needs to step up to the plate and get back on course with physical and relational health. Will you be among those who do so in our generation? Will you join the company of Daniel?

Scripture to Remember:

"You are living a brand new kind of life that is continually learning more and more of what is right..." Colossians 3:10 (TLB)

Assignment:

- Read about how food has changed since the last century (Appendix 3).

- Think about the way our culture has shifted to materialism (possessions more important than people and purpose), hedonism (if it feels good, do it...now), and narcissism (short-term pleasures of one's self and a disregard for how one's actions affect the lives of others).
- Consider ways the nurture and nutritional roles in the home are being met (or not).
- For those *really* serious about *The Good Life* (abundant living), fill out the Family System Evaluation (Appendix 4).

Start NOW! Eat a banana, apple, pear, strawberry, a cluster of grapes or some sort of fresh fruit every day. Make a smoothie in your blender out of a fresh banana, almond or rice milk (not soy milk), frozen blueberries or strawberries, a small handful of raw cashews, 2-3 dates (remove the pits!) and honey to taste. Experiment with proportions to your taste (more milk for thinner consistency or more frozen fruit for a thicker one).

*" ... test us ... see how we look compared to the other young men
who are eating the king's food.
Then make your decision in light of what you see."*

Lesson 2 – UNDERSTANDING

How it Happened – Blown Off Course

Although I stood barely tall enough to see over the table, I remember well the night my daddy brought a vegetable juicer home. We lived in Tulsa, Oklahoma, and Daddy wanted to juice the produce he enjoyed growing in our backyard garden in the city. The combination of fresh vegetable juices was foreign to me. But my parents were trying to be healthy. They took extra steps to ensure each of their children received proper nutrition, or so they thought. Beside each plate at the dinner table, vitamins sat in little dishes. Turbinado sugar was passed to put on our shredded wheat cereal with sliced bananas. Vegetables were included at lunch and suppertime meals. Now, fast-forward a few years to the next season of my life when we lived in the country.

The horses were saddled and waiting as we traded gardening clothes for cowboy boots. This was the day for cattle roundup, which meant tagging the new calves, administering immunizations, and inserting hormone pellets just under the skin of the ear in the 100 head of Angus cattle on our small family ranch. After my brother, sister and I tied up the horses from the roundup, I crawled up on the barn roof above the cattle shoot with the record book. I looked down at my mother and father as they worked the gate, trapping each one of the cattle by the neck so they could do the work that was standard practice in cattle country. These animals were being raised free range and with good foods, not in a stockyard up to their knees in manure. These animals looked beautiful. I was around 12 years old.

Growing up, I don't recall any association with people who were advocating a 100% organic lifestyle. Although I saw my daddy add food scraps to his compost pile in the corner of the garden, "stir" it and add worms to help the food scraps break down more quickly, I also saw him fight the bugs with pesticides and feed the plants with chemical fertilizers. Daddy did his best with what he knew, and as far as I know not many others were doing more to live a healthy lifestyle than were my parents. With an orchard of pear and peach trees, the 200+ pecan trees, 2 one-acre gardens, a herd of cattle, chickens, and a farm-raised catfish pond, our family experienced a bounty of fresh foods. Momma, along with my twin sister and I, canned the bounty all summer long. By the time fall arrived, there were 500+ jars in our cellar.

Momma and Daddy were my heroes, my real-to-life role models. **They did the best they could with what they knew. They gave us the best their life experiences had to offer.** *They went above and beyond in their effort to give Tina, Angela, Joe, Steve, Barb, John and me all we would need to grow to a healthy adulthood.*

What, if anything, was missing in my parents' attempt at healthy living? Is the lifestyle, modeled for us by our parents, all there is to know about healthy bodies and relationships? Can a vibrant, healthy life truly be achieved? Thank God, we can be appreciative of all efforts that were made and <u>can build upon those efforts</u> by continuing to search until we find additional answers. So, where else can we look for good role models?

How about a man who has stood the test of time, a man with roots connected to the Creator of humanity? Let's go back in history and take a look at the life of the Biblical Daniel, and do so with a more holistic approach - not just his diet, but also his spiritual relationship, human relationships, and purpose for living ... his "assignment".

"Why," you may ask, "are we talking about relationships in a course about the diet and lifestyle revealed in the life of Daniel?" First of all I would say that it is not only very important, but necessary because we are social beings. Shared sorrow is half sorrow. Shared joy is double joy. We were designed for family intimacy and responsibility, for spiritual connections, and for community living. We need group celebrations, as well as group comfort. Secondly, we need the synergy created by group participation to help us to victorious living.

Dr. Lorraine Day is a perfect example. When diagnosed with breast cancer, she changed her diet but not her **lifestyle**. For example, her connections and her stress were not addressed. The result? Her marble-sized tumor came back the size of a large softball! After addressing all components of health building, she has lived cancer free for decades.

As much as I enjoy food, I wouldn't consider myself a "foodie". I personally am more motivated (as evidenced by the dual topics of this book) to look at diet and exercise as they relate to my relationships with God, my family, my friends, and my opportunities to influence the world. It's in our DNA to live a balanced life with all the health-building components in proper proportions to the others. Dis-ease is being out-of-balance.

After we take a look at Daniel, we will explore where and why he adopted his healthy living guidelines. As you may recall, his situation had some similarities to what we face today. Since he was a captive in Babylon, he did not live in the home of his parents where strict Hebrew dietary laws were observed. He did not have their support or the support of an entire community that shared his values. He did, however, have the support of a few of his closest friends, and together they lived counter-culturally, *proving* that this lifestyle has many benefits.

In the book of Daniel, we see four main beliefs that contributed to his success:

1) **He knew <u>who he was.</u>**
   - He had accepted his family as his "assignment" in life.
   - He hadn't rejected his family of origin, thus making himself a prodigal.
   - He identified with whom God placed him.

   "... Ashpenaz ... brought into the king's service some of the Israelites from the royal family and the <u>nobility</u>."
   Daniel 1:3 (NIV, paraphrase mine)

2) **He knew <u>where he was going.</u>**
   - He accepted his responsibility (as defined by his family of origin) and humbly submitted himself to be instructed for the service.

   He was *"well informed..."* and
   "...qualified to serve in the King's palace."
   Daniel 1:4 (NIV)

3) **He knew <u>with whom he was going.</u>**
   - He was connected to others with similar "assignments."

   *"Among these were some from Judah:
   Daniel, Hananiah, Mishael and Azariah."*
   (Referring to Shadrach, Meshach, Abednego) Daniel 1:6 (NIV)

4) **He knew <u>how to empower himself to fulfill his destiny.</u>**
   - He understood His Creator's design for healthy living.

   "But Daniel resolved not to defile himself with the royal food and wine; and he asked the chief official for

> *permission not to defile himself this way. . . . Please test your servants for ten days: Give us nothing but vegetables to eat and water to drink. Then compare our appearance with that of the young men who eat the royal food, and treat your servants in accordance with what you see." Daniel 1:8, 12, 13 (NIV)*

This wasn't something new to Daniel, as evidenced by his description in verse four: He was *"without any physical defect, handsome, showing aptitude for every kind of learning, and quick to understand."*

The Result?

Of the Biblical Daniel, it was said that he *"looked better and more robust,"* had *"skill and knowledge in both books and life,"* was *"gifted in understanding,"* was *"found far superior"* and *"ten times better"* than those who were not following the Creator's design. This young man knew little of brain fog, acne, confusion, excess weight, meaningless or dissatisfying life, bad relationships, or exhaustion (Daniel 1, NIV). *Wow!* What are we waiting for? **Let's join Daniel!** Although we will discuss relationships later in Lesson 5, let's begin by **focusing on the diet**.

Who decides what we humans should eat anyway? Let me answer that with this illustration: I bought a wool sweater for my husband a few Christmases ago. As my husband requested, I washed the sweater before he wore it. Unfortunately, I didn't read the manufacturer's guidelines for the garment and I shrunk it to the size a five-year-old boy would wear. ("Sorry, Sweetheart!") If I had paid attention to the manufacturer's advice, the sweater would have been in great condition and wearable for my husband.

So, who decides what humans should eat? The answer is clear: our "Manufacturer". Our Manufacturer or Creator had a plan in mind when He made humans. He knows what fuel will provide a source for high performance, peace, and rejuvenation. It is found in Genesis 1 of the "Owner's Manual" (The Bible) and says,

> *"Then God said, 'I give you every seed-bearing plant on the face of the whole earth and every tree that has fruit with seed in it. They will be yours for food. And to all the beasts of the earth and all the birds of the air and all the creatures that move on the ground—everything that has the breath of life in it—I give every green plant for food.' And it was so. God saw all that he had made, and it was very good."*
> Genesis 1:29-31(NIV)

For further study, I have provided additional commentary for some scriptures with reference to dietary guidelines in Appendix 5. I want to bring clarity to these particular scriptures, as they occasionally confuse people. Bottom line, we know that Daniel ate fruits, vegetables, nuts, seeds, and whole grains; we know that he drank water. (Believe it or not, I've met people in our culture who think that fruit punch, fruit-flavored candies, and fruit-flavored cereals are a good source of fruit for their children. If that's you, I'm not making fun; I'm just stating that we need to get some things clarified here.) What you don't know can harm you! What you don't know <u>can</u> **kill** you!

> | The Creator's plan worked for Daniel, has worked for many through the ages, and will work for us today! |

> *"My people are DESTROYED for lack of knowledge."*
> Hosea 4:6 (KJV)

> *"... get wisdom. **Though it cost all you have**, get understanding."*
> Proverbs 4:7 (NIV, emphasis mine)

There is food that kills and food that brings life. So, let's take a minute to talk about the difference between "real food" and "junk food".

What is the difference between REAL food and JUNK food?

	Real Food contains these elements	Junk Food contains these elements
Glucose	Yes	Yes
Protein	Yes	1/2
Fatty Acids	Yes	No (100% de-natured)
Minerals	Yes	No
Enzymes	Yes	No
Water	Yes	No - 1/2
Toxins	No	Yes

Toxins are defined as any substance that is foreign to the body, which the body cannot use in any way for life maintaining purposes. These toxins are, in fact, poisonous and detrimental to the body, costing the body energy and nutrition to eliminate them. When toxins are consumed, the body attempts to eliminate them. This elimination process oftentimes uses the adrenal glands to speed up the process. Rather than using the adrenals for their intended use, i.e. fight or flight situations, the adrenals are being used as emergency hazardous material collectors. Thus, many people in our society are experiencing **adrenal burnout**. Consequently, when they need the adrenals to kick in and provide extra energy, they just cannot.

> If food is prepared inappropriately, then it will "rob" what it needs from other parts of the body to be able to process that food through the body system.

So, **real** food becomes **junk** food when it has been processed, oxidized, cooked limp, laced with additives, or grown in depleted soil that cannot provide nutrition for the plant.

What Happens When Foods Are Processed

> Have you noticed that processed foods are typically dry, thus causing people to drink a lot of liquid with their meals? This dilutes the digestive juices, rendering them less effective in the digestion process. Foods eaten in their natural state tend to have nutrient-dense liquids in them. Therefore, try to drink *between* meals rather that with your meal.

Essential nutrients are stripped from the food via:

- Overheating (anything above 105 degrees)
- Oxidation (When the skin is cut on produce the break down process begins. Example: Apples turn brown after being cut.)
- Processing and discarding (Food is packaged in nature with enzymes needed for digestion and assimilation in the body. Discarded enzymes slow down this process. Peeling cucumbers, carrots, and potatoes is an example.)
- Addition of toxic materials (A few examples include herbicides, pesticides, preservatives, color, flavors, enhancers, growth hormones, antibiotics.)

Ten times better!

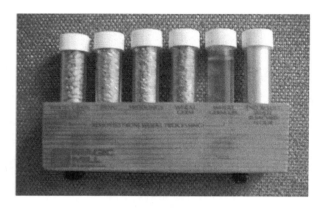

(Pictured from left to right are vials filled with whole grain wheat and the break down of the different components found therein: whole grain unrefined wheat, bran, middling, wheat germ, wheat germ oil, and the white flour which is left after all these nutrients are removed.)

As you have seen in the picture above, to increase shelf life of flour, wheat berries are stripped of bran, middling, wheat germ, and oils, leaving only the refined white flour. *"But,"* you say, *"I eat foods that are **enriched!**"* That's similar thinking to the man who was robbed of his clothing, money, watch, and other possessions, but was given back his wallet and underwear and told, "Now you're OK! You're good-to-go." (In other words, "Now, you're *enriched*!") What a farce! We wouldn't tolerate that with our clothing and other belongings. Why would we tolerate it with our foods? Note: The longer the shelf-life of the food due to processing and preservatives, the more likely that our lives will be shorter.

God designed our foods in a complete package with all the nutrients needed to digest and assimilate them to a usable state. When foods are robbed of any part of the "package," they become **nutrient robbed**, rather than **nutrient packed**, because the body develops a need to draw those stripped nutrients from other parts of the body and assimilate them.

Empower Your Purpose: The Daniel FEAST! - Lesson Two

The pictures here illustrate what we have been talking about. One is a raw carrot that sprouted to create new LIFE! If we planted it, we would have more carrots on our carrot plant. The other is a picture of some "fast food" that we purchased for an illustration. We purchased only bread and meat without the tomato, lettuce, onion, pickle and  condiments. In this picture, taken at the time of this printing, it is five years old and looks the same as the day we purchased it. If we plant it, it won't grow hamburger bushes. There is NO LIFE in it. Although a crude way of putting it, would it be accurate to say that it has been *embalmed* and that it is DEAD food being

served in a casket? Do you trust that to give life to your body? Isn't it obvious, from the picture of the sprouting carrot, that the life-giving force found in living foods can be our best medicine? Life begets life. Chemical symptom-removers create more symptoms. If you need a refresher on that concept, watch the drug commercials during the 5:00 p.m. news cast.

Our Body's Fuel

Have we assumed personal responsibility for the health of our body (God's temple) and the health of our family?

> *"What? Know ye not that your body is the temple of the Holy Spirit? And ye are not your own, for ye are bought with a price. Therefore, GLORIFY GOD WITH YOUR BODY."*
> I Corinthians 6:19, 20 (KJV)

Let's compare body fuel to car fuel. You wouldn't put water into the gas tank, syrup in the oil pan, or use fruit-flavored punch instead of windshield wiper fluid and expect it to function according to the manufacturer's design. What about your body's fuel? Some people think that they can put <u>anything</u> into their bodies and get a high level of function, health and beauty. Many ingest stimulants as fuel, focusing only on the present need for energy and clear thinking. These stimulants (caffeine, salt, sugars, and refined foods) may "get you going" and make you highly productive at the time; however, for long-term health, we must assess the damage done after the initial benefit of pleasure and instant energy wears off. It's kind of like this: consuming caffeine, salt, sugars, or refined foods can leave one as physically out of control as a car being hit by an 18-wheeler truck. The little car will go really fast, but 1) is it really in control of itself? and 2) what damage was done to the bumper when it got hit? These energy drinks with massive doses of caffeine in them *really* concern me.

> These stimulants (caffeine, salt, sugars, and refined foods) may "get you going" and make you highly productive at the time; however, for long-term health, we must assess the damage done after the initial benefit of pleasure and instant energy wears off.

When <u>any</u> stimulants are used (but especially those energy drinks that are primarily stimulation), the adrenals kick in to do their damage control by revving up the system to get those toxins out! So, a part of the body that was designed for fight or flight emergencies is being called upon for everyday functionality. Thus, many Americans are experiencing the exhaustion of **adrenal burnout** as the emergency back-up plan of adrenal support is shot. Therefore, there is a need to crowd out the toxic foods by feeding their adrenals nutrient-dense foods to get them built back up again.

> **THINK ABOUT IT: Eternal life in heaven is not dependent upon what we eat. Jesus' death on the cross, as our substitute, paid the legal price for our redemption from the kingdom of darkness and into fellowship with our Heavenly Father. The food issue is about *abundant living*.**

> *"'Everything is permissible for me' - but not everything is beneficial.
> 'Everything is permissible for me' - but I will not be mastered
> by anything."*
> I Corinthians 6:12 (NIV)

Basically, you are what you…

- Eat
- Digest
- Assimilate

Eat foods in their natural forms (not processed or cooked) as the Creator made them. You see, God put into each food type the components it would need to not only digest, but also assimilate it into the areas of the body where it is needed. **You can eat the right foods prepared the wrong way and still be self-defeating, because the enzymes that render foods useable for digestion and assimilation into the body have been cut away and discarded or overheated and killed.** Take a look at the chart below for percentages of nutrients lost through different types of food preparation.

Hierarchy of Food Preparation

Raw & Whole   ➢ Ideal consumption of fruits, vegetables, nuts, seeds, and grains.
Juiced (Consumed Immediately)   ➢ Minimal nutrient loss (However, oxidation kills enzymes when oxygen mixes in.)
Dehydrated or Dried   ➢ 2%-5% nutrient loss   ➢ Must be dried without chemicals or additives (such as sulfur-dioxide found in commercial dried fruit, except raisins).
Freshly Picked and Immediately Frozen   ➢ 5%-30% nutrient loss

Steamed ➢ 15%-60% nutrient loss ➢ Veggies must remain crispy. If limp, they're cooked.	
Cooked ➢ 40%-100% nutrient loss (depends on how long item was cooked) ➢ Includes: baked, broiled, grilled, over-steamed, & home canned	
Microwaved ➢ 90%-99% nutrient loss	
Cooked Leftovers ➢ 100% nutrient loss (oxidation and heating over 105 degrees)	
Commercially Canned Foods ➢ 90%-99% nutrient loss (Metal or glass, due to oxidation and overheating)	
Fried Foods ➢ 90%-99% nutrient loss ➢ Harmful to the body (oxidation, heat, and fat)	
Foods With Additives ➢ 100% nutrient loss ➢ Added toxins	

"Give me understanding and I will obey your instructions;
I will put them into practice with all my heart."
Psalm 119:34 (NLT)

When we understand how dead and processed foods have a negative affect on our well being, on our future and on the future of those our lives touch, we are more empowered to make healthier lifestyle choices.

Scripture to Remember:

"'Everything is permissible for me' - but not everything is beneficial. 'Everything is permissible for me' - but I will not be mastered by anything." I Corinthians 6:12 (NIV)

Assignment: Look up the definitions for "Good" and "Bad" and come prepared to share your findings.

Start NOW! Eat a salad with dark lettuce, field greens, or spinach (not iceberg lettuce) every day. Lean towards Italian or vinaigrette dressings and steer away from dairy and sugar laden dressings. Choose whole grain breads or crackers to eat with it ("whole grain," not "unbleached wheat"). For those of you who know you must steer away from gluten, try breads and pizza crusts made out of whole grain rice rather than processed white rice.

" ... test us ... see how we look compared to the other young men who are eating the king's food. Then make your decision in light of what you see."

Lesson 3 – SHIFTING

More Paradigms for Transitioning Back on Course

I was born in Tulsa, Oklahoma, and lived there until I was 9 years old. We then moved to a small town in northeast Oklahoma to live on the family ranch my parents purchased from my grandfather. It was summer time. Because our Tulsa home had sold and our new home was still being built, we "camped out" for the summer in our barn. Daddy put down fresh hay on one side of the barn that became our "bedroom". He even tacked a black plastic tarp above our cots to protect us from the drips from the tin roof when it rained. (He said with a mischievous grin, "You always wanted a canopy bed; well, here you go!") He also stretched a rope across the large open doors so we could get a breeze and keep the horses out. A large barrel of tools stood on one side of the door and Daddy's welding bench on the other. The "living room" consisted of a few lawn chairs in a circle and a picnic table sat next to them where we ate our meals. I'll bet I was the only girl in the county who could eat breakfast in the "breakfast nook" while her daddy welded corner posts and gates for the new fences in the "living room"!

Every day my siblings and I would go over to the new house and watch whatever builder was working. There was an on-going joke between the carpenters and the plumbers about who was the "nastiest," as they all chewed tobacco. Occasionally it would run down their chin and drip on their bib overalls. We were told to leave alone the cups that they spit in. (We didn't really have to be told that!) This was my first experience with this substance. I saw it again when I attended a rodeo in our small community. The youth would congregate behind the bleachers and check out one another's boots, hats, or latest belt or belt buckle. It was there, too, that I saw different ones take (one of many) country boy's rites of passage and try a cigarette or a chew of tobacco. Somehow that first drag or chew didn't produce the delight it promised. They coughed out the smoke, and oftentimes swallowed some of the chew, eyes watering and faces turning a bit green. Sometimes a run for the cover of darkness and sounds of losing the hamburger, fries, and shake they had just consumed followed this new experience.

That same summer I had my first experience with carbonated beverages. My youngest brother, John, played Pee Wee baseball on our small town team. My twin sister and I would work in the Dilly Wagon serving refreshments during the game. Afterwards, some generous fan would offer to pay for soft drinks for the entire team. My sister and I put the ice in the cups, filled them with the dark colored beverage, and topped them off once the fizz settled down. I had never seen this drink before, much less tasted it. When we got the cups all ready for the team, the adult supervising the Dilly Wagon offered me one of the cold drinks. I thanked her and took a sip. OH MY GOODNESS! It <u>burned</u> all the way down, and the fizz bubbled up into my sinus cavity! This was NOT pleasant! I was used to milk and water and an occasional fruit-flavored drink. I'd never experienced anything like this. But here came the team. The ball players all grabbed their soft drinks with obvious delight. I wanted to belong. It looked as if they really enjoyed it. It must be good. "I'll give it another try," I thought.

With each of these things – smoking, chewing tobacco, carbonated beverages – **there is a need to acquire a taste**. When these things are not in your diet or are not the "norm" for you, it takes time for them to become enjoyable. Can the same be done with things that are <u>good</u> for you?

I believe the answer is, "Yes!" While it does take time for the body to be cleansed of toxic foods and for tastes to change, these "good for you" foods will become the foods that your body craves and that satisfy your dietary needs … in time. In this lesson we will identify a myriad of food options for building health and some transitional foods that aren't optimal but that are better than more toxic junk food, which can help us make the transition. We will also discuss what to do if you have difficulty with the idea of adding these foods to your diet, or perhaps even have a nightmarish fear of changing your current diet.

As we begin this lesson, I'd like for you to take a few minutes to highlight the foods listed below that are currently in your diet, even if you only eat them at special holiday times. Then take a minute to cheer for anything and everything you are contributing to your good health. (If you only have a few, don't worry. We won't despise small beginnings! Remember, there is no condemnation. We've all been blown off course in one area or another. We'll just identify how, gather the tools we need, and get back on course!)

Nutrient-Dense Foods

Fruits	Vegetables
Apples	Alfalfa Sprouts
Apricots	Artichokes
Bananas	Asparagus
Blackberries	Beets/Beet Greens
Blueberries	Bok Choy
Boysenberries	Broccoli
Cranberries	Brussels Sprouts
Cherries	Cabbage
Dates	Carrots

Elderberries	Cauliflower
Figs (dried or fresh)	Celery
Gooseberries	Chives
Grapefruit	Collards
Grapes (red, green, raisins)	Corn on the Cob
Kiwi	Cucumbers
Lemons	Endive
Limes	Green Beans
Mandarin Oranges	Kale
Mangos	Leeks
Melon, Cantaloupe	Lettuce (except iceberg)
Melon, Cassava	Mushrooms
Melon, Honeydew	Onions
Melon, Watermelon	Parsley
Nectarines	Peas (green, snow, sugar snap)
Oranges / Tangerines	Peppers
Papayas	Potatoes
Passion Fruit	Radishes
Pears	Sea Kelp
Pineapples	Spinach
Raspberries	Squash
Strawberries	Swiss Chard
	Tomatoes
	Turnips
	Yams
	Watercress

Healthy Fats/Oils	Sweeteners
Avocado	Apples
	Dates
Cold Pressed Natural:	Figs
Coconut Oil/ Butter	Pears
Extra Virgin Olive Oil	Pineapple
Flaxseed Oil	Raisins

Ten times better!

Grape Seed	Raw Agave Nectar
Sesame Oil	Raw Honey
Sunflower Oil	Raw Maple Syrup

Beverages	**Cereals/Breads**
Dried Green Drinks	All Bran Cereal
Dried Veggie Drinks	Bagels, Whole Grain
Herbal Teas	Bran Muffins
Purified Water	Breads, Whole Grain
Freshly Squeezed Fruit	English Muffins
Fresh Veggie Juice	Grape Nuts™
Fresh Green Drinks	Hamburger Buns
Smoothies	Manna Bread™ (frozen raw)
Nut Milks	Oatmeal
	Pita Bread
	Rice, Brown or Wild
	Tortillas
Those of you who are gluten intolerant will need to adapt this list according to your health care provider or natural health care advisor's instructions.	Uncle Sam's Cereal™
	Wheat Crackers
	NOTE: Look for 100% whole grains and high fiber, no sugar, sprouted, or multi-grain cereals

Seasonings/Spices and Miscellaneous	
Almond Extract	Herbamare™
Apple Cider Vinegar (raw unpasteurized)	Miso
Braggs Liquid Amino™ (raw)	Paprika

Celtic Sea Salt	Raw Almond Butter
Cayenne Pepper	Raw Carob Powder
Chili Powder	Raw Sesame Seed Butter
Cumin	Sun-dried Tomatoes
Dulse Flakes	Vanilla Extract
Flax Oil	Young Thai Coconut
Garlic	
Ginger Root	

According to Paul Zane Piltzer, **cow's milk and milk bi-products** cause allergies, gas, constipation, obesity, cancer, heart disease, infectious diseases, and osteoporosis. I would encourage you to research "The Dairy Deception" on line or purchase his book, *Wellness Revolution*, to see what else he has to say about the conditions many dairy cows are in, the amount of white blood cells (pus) the USDA allows to be in the drinking milk, what the bovine growth hormone (BGH) is doing to the age of menarche and breast sizes of today's young girls and how that is producing cancer in them as they age.

Soybean Products have received much acceptance in the United States as an alternative to animal proteins. However, in the countries that consume them successfully, they are combined with a mineral-rich fish broth to assist with digestion and assimilation (unlike the use in America). Thus, many experts recommend using nut milks and nut meats instead of soy products.

Note: It is best to get **protein** in the form of amino acids in vegetarian sources. However, if preferred, purchase meat, fish, and poultry from a health food store to avoid chemical contaminates. A palm-sized portion is recommended; even better still would be to cut the meat in bite-size or smaller pieces and use as a seasoning, as is often seen in Asian foods.

Ten times better!

Protein Sources

Animal *(Transitional foods)*	Vegetarian *(Nuts, Seeds, & Fruit)*
Chicken Breast (free range)	Almonds
Cornish Hen	Avocado
Ground Turkey Breast	Beechnuts
Ground Chicken	Brazil Nuts
Eggs (Vegetarian Fed)	Cashews
Fish:	Coconut
Bass	Chia Seeds
Bluefish	Flax Seeds
Cod	Goji Berries
Flounder	Hemp Seeds
Haddock	Lentils
Halibut	Macadamia Nuts
Mackerel	Olives
Mahi Mahi	Pecans
Orange Roughy	Pine Nuts
Red Snapper	Pistachio Nuts
Salmon	Pumpkin Seeds
Sardines	Sesame Seeds
Trout	Sunflower Seeds
Tuna	Walnuts (English & Black)
Whitefish	
	Legumes
	Brown beans
	Black beans
	Red beans
	Lentils
	White beans

Transitional foods: This is the name we've assigned to foods that aren't nutrient dense but that are typically familiar and that aid in the transition to a healthier lifestyle. These foods are not ideal for building health. For example, salad dressings that you like or that your family likes may have the wrong kinds of fats, dairy and sugar; but if you want or feel a need for them to help your family learn to eat salads, then relax and realize you can swap out better-for-you dressings in another step. Unless you are deathly ill, you have time to make these changes in a gentle progression. Relax and enjoy the journey. You don't have to do it perfectly to be effective. **Focus on making progress** no matter how large or small the steps are. Eating with people who have already made these changes will help you stay motivated and contribute energy into your transition.

The next section is one of **the most important** ones in this teaching. Somehow, somewhere, we got the idea that if something doesn't taste good to us, we shouldn't eat it. Period. End of discussion. Thus, adding new and different-tasting things to our diets (some of which we've  never even seen or heard of) is intimidating and often seems repulsive. A very important step in this health-building journey is a **paradigm shift** from "If it feels good do it, and if it doesn't, don't!" to "If it's good for me, do it and grow to appreciate it (and maybe even **love** it!)."

"Good" and "Bad"

Webster's 1828 dictionary provides definitions that correlate with building health. I like the definitions of the words *good* and *bad* that I found there. (Last week's assignment comes into play here. What definitions did you find for "good" and "bad"?)

"Good" = fresh, unspoiled, uncontaminated, ample, adequate, sufficient, healthy and strong

"Bad" = not pleasant, unfavorable, unfit, inadequate, immoral, causing injury, harmful, ill, in poor health

> You don't have to do it perfectly to be effective. **Focus on making progress** no matter how large or small the steps are.

Based on these definitions, we see that it would be helpful to stop calling foods "good" that are creating disease, causing the amputation of limbs, denying meaningful lives with family and friends, producing pain and suffering, and pulling others away from serving Adonai to care for us. That models the exact opposite of abundant life to a lost and dying world! That is immoral. I don't believe anyone says or even thinks before eating a double-bacon cheeseburger and super-sized box of fries, "I think I'll see how many people I can inconvenience with my illnesses today." No. We aren't maturely looking past the enjoyment of the moment to the consequences in our lives or in the lives of those close to us; but we must!

"It is BETTER to spend your time at funerals than festivals for you ARE going to die, and it is a GOOD thing to think about while there is still time. Sorrow is BETTER than laughter, for sadness has a refining influence on us. Yes, a wise man thinks much of death, while the fool thinks only of having a good time now." Ecclesiastes 7:2-4 (TLB)

Acquiring a Taste for what is Truly Good

*"Woe to those who call **good** bad, and **bad** good..."*
Isaiah 5:20 (personal paraphrase)

Paradigm shift: In order to gain health, one must eat primarily for fuel and healing rather than temporary comfort and socializing. This will allow you to enjoy a lifetime filled with energy and quality. Times of feasting and celebration are very important. But, for maximum health, they must not be the *primary focus* for eating.

If one can <u>acquire a taste</u> for activities that seem fun or "good," but that increase the potential for harm like:

- Smoking tobacco
- Chewing tobacco
- Consuming alcohol (excessively)
- Sniffing drugs
- IV Drugs

... then one can <u>acquire a taste</u> for activities that seem boring or "bad" at first, but actually help you in the end, such as:

- Relaxation Techniques
- Light Exercise
- Healthy Connections
- Education & Mentorship
- Spiritual Enrichment

Likewise, if one can <u>acquire a taste</u> for foods which the majority of society has learned to enjoy, but harm you later, such as:

- Hydrogenated fats
- Refined sugars
- Processed foods
- Soda
- Caffeinated beverages

… then one can <u>acquire a taste</u> for foods that may seem to taste "bad" at first, but begin to taste great as they become familiar and help your body in the end, such as:

- Fruits & vegetables
- Nuts, seeds, olives
- Whole grain breads
- Pure water
- Honey

Therefore, to <u>acquire a taste</u> we must do three things:

1. **Try it.** We can't learn to like something if we won't put it in our mouths!

2. **Try it again. Connect the dots** between the things that bring us harm and the things that bring us life! We must think about the bigger picture and how our actions affect others, our service to our Heavenly Father, and our part in history. We must tell our minds to grow up and  do what is in the best interest of our bodies and our responsibilities. As our bodies cleanse, we will acquire a taste for these foods because they are the Creator's design. The other foods are non-foods and a lie of the evil one to cut our lives short.

3. **Meditate on the benefits.** Now it is a familiar taste to our bodies, and the body recognizes the benefits. Example: clear thinking, positive outlook, energy for creativity, synergy in relationships, beautiful skin and hair.

"You made my body, Lord;
now give me sense to heed Your laws."
Psalms 119:73 (TLB)

"Your laws are always fair,
help me to understand them and I shall live."
Psalm 119:144 (TLB)

> As our bodies cleanse, our tastes will change. It will be easier and easier to acquire a taste for nutrient-dense foods. We will find that we are enjoying foods we never dreamed we would.

The next section may seem out of place for a beginner's course on the *Daniel Lifestyle*; however, I wanted to include it for three reasons. First, there are bound to be people taking this course who have already made the connection between lifestyle and health, who are ready for a more serious focus on reclaiming their health and increasing their vibrancy. This information will help those folks understand the different types of cleansing and why one type is more effective than another.

Today, many churches are calling for "Daniel Fasts" and fasts during the Lent season, which help people break away from activities and foods that are bogging them down and hindering spiritual productivity and growth. Daniel fasts and Daniel diets are synonymous in this work and refer to a singular fsocus on one's diet, as opposed to the Daniel Lifestyle, which would include other health-building components as well. Physical cleansing through fasting can be disease preventing in a similar way that cleaning out clutter from one's home can prevent a fire from a frayed extension cord or allergies from all the dust or mold.

Second, the body repairs itself nightly. We can make some <u>simple</u> adjustments that will maximize the effectiveness of the cleansing that takes place while we sleep and, just as easily, we can do things to sabotage that process.

Third, a big breakfast to fuel your day may actually slow you down. Let's take a look at the next two charts.

Body Cleansing According to Energy Economics

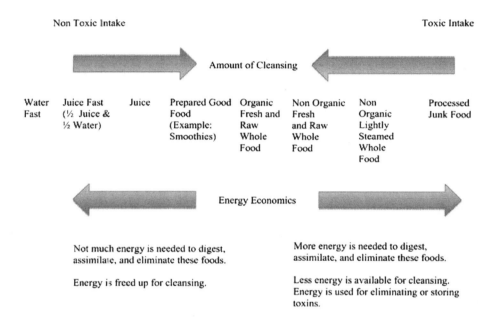

The Water Fast: This is the most difficult and will probably need to be done when there are low demands on one's time and energy. No energy is being used for digestion, assimilation, and elimination; therefore, maximum energy is available for cleansing and repair work in the body.

The "Juice Fast" and "Juice Only": These are freshly made juices, not ones pre-made and packed from the store. Little energy is being used for digestion, assimilation, and elimination; therefore, much energy is available for cleansing and repair work. If you add ground flax to the juice, that puts it in the next category - as the flax will take longer to digest and assimilate than the juice by itself. (It is helpful to use ground flax or flax seed oil when one has blood sugar issues. It slows down the digestion of the sweeter juices.)

Prepared "Good Food": These foods are different than processed foods in that they are in their whole form as found in nature, not discarding any part nor consuming after oxidation has opportunity to destroy enzymes. However, since they have been ground up for you (such as in a smoothie), the energy needed to chew is freed up for cleansing or repair.

Organic Fresh and Raw Whole Food: These foods are free from the toxic materials that send our bodies into a "fight or flight – DANGER! DANGER! – get-that-out-of-here!" mode.

Non-organic Fresh and Raw Food: The foods themselves are good for you, but the toxic chemicals they have been treated with slow down the detoxing process as more toxin are being put into the body.

Non-organic Lightly Steamed Whole Food: These foods are still crunchy and have nutrition in them, albeit, less than those totally raw. Again, the foods themselves are good for you, but the toxic chemicals they have been treated with, slow down the detoxing process as more toxin are being put into the body and some enzymes have been killed in the heating process.

Junk Food: These foods have been cooked until they are limp, processed by cutting the vitamin rich skins away, or denatured through oxidation by preparing them hours ahead of time. Many of them have been fried in oils that change into harmful substances when heated. Thus, energy must be used to deal with the immediate problems of what was just eaten rather than cleaning house else where in the body.

Think about it: If you see that you need to do some spring cleaning, you don't want to begin it on laundry day; especially if your three college age sons or daughters bring home all their laundry to do that weekend!

Remember to eat primarily for fuel and healing, rather than for temporary comfort and socializing, so that you may enjoy pleasures that last!

Energy Economics

What does it cost your body (in energy) to digest and assimilate the food you are eating, such as processed food, meat, grain, fat, fruits, vegetables, and juices?

Digestion TimeTable

Food	Approximate Hours of Digestion
Processed foods	Unknown (over 10)
Meats (red, white, well-done)	7-9
Meats (fish, other)	4-6
Nuts, Grains & Seeds	4-5
Raw Vegetables & Starch	2-3
Raw Fruits	1
Melons	Immediately - ½ hour
Juicing	Immediately - ½ hour

After reviewing these two charts, ask yourself these questions:

1. What are some things I can do to maximize the effectiveness of the cleansing repair work during night hours?
2. Why would this be effective?
3. What are some things I may be doing to hinder that process and why?

4. During a work or school day, when one has a presentation or test the first part of the day and has eaten a large breakfast, what happens to the energy needed for digestion and brainpower? (Check out www.paulnison.com for more information on the "Daylight Diet".)

In a health-building lifestyle, the "fast" that occurs during sleep could be modified to include a morning juice fast (or juicing for breakfast), thus extending the time of repairing and cleansing, or reserving energy for a test or business presentation. If the demands of the day begin to wind down in the evening, one could benefit greatly by having the bigger meal of the day around 5:30 or 6:00. Doing so would allow the body to use energy for digestion before sleep occurs, saving energy for the cleansing and repair work of the sleep hours. Our culture tends to go to bed on a full stomach, minimizing the effectiveness of those night hours. Does it make sense now why many people can't get to sleep, or go to sleep only to wake up before it's time, or experience leg syndrome or night sweats? Then they wake up feeling like they've been run over by a truck – achy, low energy and stumbling towards the coffee pot.

What does it cost your body in energy to participate in an activity or in a lifestyle, such as sports, a stressful project, late work nights, over-committed time, and bad relationships? A focus on *energy economics* could be an eye opener for your productivity and joy.

> *"There is a way that seemeth right unto a man, but the end thereof are the ways of death."* Proverbs 14:12 (KJV)

THINK ABOUT IT: Are we fueling our bodies with nutrient rich or nutrient robbing foods? Are we eating *primarily* for fuel and healing or fun, comfort and socialization? Are we working with our design or against it?

Transitioning: The Daniel FEAST

So what does a dietary day in the life of the transitional generation look like? Well, it's very simple. Since the average American spends 91 cents out of every dollar on processed foods, and Americans are primarily "red meat and potato" people, we are going to simply focus on *adding living foods to the diet*. No counting this or that, reading labels or listening to long lectures. Instead, simply ask yourself the following questions:

1. Have I had any fresh fruit today?
2. Have I had any raw vegetables today?
   (No iceberg lettuce, but a salad made of dark leafy greens.)
3. Have I had any raw nuts, seeds or legumes?
4. Have I had purified water?
5. Have I had any whole grain breads or cereals?

Think about these key words:

    Fresh   Raw   Bright   Variety   SIMPLE

Eat a banana and raw walnuts, an orange and raw cashews, an apple with nut butter or dipped in honey (like a caramel apple), a handful of grapes, strawberries and raw pecans, a few almonds with a carrot. These are some great combinations. (Start a fad. Make it cool to walk around eating these!)

Every day, eat a salad; don't miss. (Salad is more than iceberg lettuce, a couple pieces of tomato and a sprinkle of processed cheese. No need to ever be bored with salads! There is no end to the amazing blends of veggies that taste great and have such eye appeal. They just look like LIFE!) While you're at it, start saving your money to buy a juicer. In the meantime, use your blender. Most everyone has one. If you don't, the little bullet blender works great for making healthy smoothies. Start with a fresh fruit and date smoothie (being sure to remove the date pits). Pears are also a great sweetener. If one prefers it sweeter than that, use honey or agave nectar for a period of time.

If you usually make your smoothies with cow's milk, then substitute unsweetened almond milk instead. You're off to a great start! See, it isn't that hard. And it's fun that *lasts!* Remember, there's fun that kills, robs, and destroys, and there's fun that gives life! You choose.

> *"The thief comes only to steal and kill and destroy; I have come that they may have life, and have it to the full."* John 10:10 (NIV)

There are additional things one can do to increase energy and build health, but this is a super place to start. Once you get your juicer, begin juicing first thing in the morning–before coffee, bagels and cream cheese, sugar cereal, or the "McMorning Muffin".

Ten times better!

The "Signature Drink" we encourage people to juice consists of <u>five carrots</u>, <u>one apple</u> and <u>one lemon</u>. Wash them all in an apple cider vinegar wash. **Important: remove the apple seeds, which contain cyanide.** It's okay to juice the lemon seeds and skin as well. If the carrot taste is too strong for you at first, no problem; just add more apple and less carrot the next time. If the lemon is too strong for you, use half or try it without next time.

Empower Your Purpose: The Daniel FEAST! - Lesson Three

> NOTE: A juicing demonstration would be good during this lesson if anyone in the group has a juicer. Suggested recipe: 5 large carrots, 1 apple, and 1 lemon. When you get used to that recipe, make the same drink and this time add 2 stalks of kale to the next drink.
>
> In your next juicing session, add a half-inch piece of ginger and a handful of parsley - for cholesterol issues - to the main recipe.
>
> The next step in your juicing journey would be to try a juice my husband and I drink if we think we may have trouble sleeping. It consists of just two ingredients. Juice 2 stalks of celery and one apple for a deep and restful sleep.

The point is to **get going**. This will get the acid and alkaline balance shifting in your body so that, eventually, your tastes will begin to change. As your body cleanses and begins to recognize (and crave) the healthy foods it was designed to love, add some dinosaur kale or regular kale (a couple leaves) to the above drink. On the ANDI scale for nutrition, kale scores the highest points (1,000) and is a great way to get extra "green" nutrients in the body. ANDI (short for *Aggregate Nutrient Density Index*) is the brainchild of author, MD, and founder of Whole Foods Market's Eat Right America, Dr. Joel Fuhrman. If your store doesn't carry kale, don't worry about it. There are other deep-colored greens that are nutrient dense, but be sure to ask your produce personnel which ones are best for juicing; some of them are HOT. (Ask me how I know. ☺)

During this time, begin to **crowd out** the red meat with salmon or baked chicken. Even better, begin to add nuts, seeds and sprouted or cooked beans to your diet.

> As your body cleanses, it begins to recognize (and crave) the healthy foods it was designed to love.

Ten times better!

If you are ready to nutrient pack your body with juices, but can't adjust your lifestyle to accommodate fresh juicing just yet, I would suggest that you tap into The Hallelujah Diet® resources and order one of the many flavors from Barley Max® (Premier Raw Food For Maximum Nutrition). Don't forget a personal hand mixer so this can be taken anywhere. (I have a little bag that I take with me when I have a day on the road. It carries my purified water, green drink powder, some fruit/veggie/nut snacks and my mini mixer.)

> *"Give me understanding. Then I will listen to Your Word and obey it with all my heart."* Psalm 119:34 (NLV)

NOTE: Just click on the banner ad for the HDiet on our website (www.MAKINGthyme.com). It will link you directly with to The Hallelujah Diet® and in so doing, it will let them know that you heard about their products and programs from us. If you prefer to call, you can keep that connection between *The Daniel FEAST* and The Hallelujah Diet® by calling our Toll-Free number 1 (855) 414.1331.

Wouldn't it be great if more churches adapted a similar concept of encouragement by having a weekly health focus - health tips scrolling on the screen, green drink options at the café, healthy snacks and meals for events? Feasting is God's idea. We don't need to condemn it; just do it *right!* When we are fully fueled, we can better fulfill our ministry opportunities. Keep watch on our website (www.MAKINGthyme.com) for developing opportunities for your school, church, or other community environments.

Daily Lifestyle

Below is a wonderful example of an optimal daily routine adapted from *The Hallelujah Diet* and is consistent with the Daniel lifestyle we teach:

6:00 a.m. Arise and drink 1st 8 oz. green drink (instead of coffee)

6:15 to 6:45 a.m. Exercise (Exercise contributes in many, many ways - including improved mood, elimination, better sleep, weight management, and enhanced function of lymph systems - to name a few.)

6:45 a.m. Hygiene and dressing for the day

7:30 a.m. Leave for work and school

10:00 a.m. Freshly made carrot, lemon, and apple juice. (This suggested signature drink helps people acquire a taste for fresh juices, and replaces the soda, candy or more coffee that is generally needed by this time.)

11:30 a.m. 2nd Green Drink (Nutrient packing; the body satisfies the energy demands needed for the day.)

12:00 p.m. Salad (Scour the Internet for a variety of delicious salad ideas. Just make sure they are "good-for-you" salads, filled with nutrient-dense ingredients and not bad fats or processed ingredients.)

3:00 p.m. Beet drink (Beets are wonderful liver cleansers. If you aren't in a position to access fresh juice, there are beet powders available. See page 46 for ordering information. My husband and I keep canisters in our respective work environments for this purpose. A little inexpensive mini hand mixer does the trick for a quick mid-afternoon pick-me-up.)

5:30 p.m. 3rd Green Drink

6:00 p.m. Salad, baked potato or pasta loaded with veggies. If you are transitioning from a heavy red meat diet, this would be a good time to add a small portion of chicken, salmon or other types of fish.

Eat nothing more after dinner so your digestion will be complete before you retire for the night. Drinking between meals prevents the digestion juices from being diluted. A nutrient-dense diet is so full of juicy foods that we don't need as much water as those on the typical American diet of processed foods and toxins.

If you feel the need for more chewing, you could have some fresh fruit or fruit leathers along with a few nuts for one of your snacks. Carrot sticks and almonds are also quite nice together. Hummus and "crackers" are a favorite healthier snack for many. (We make our crackers in the dehydrator with various nuts, flax and seasonings.)

If you are used to eating ice cream or other sweets, then a smoothie is a great replacement. There are some fabulous recipes for nutrient-dense, good-for-you cookies, brownies and fudge that *easily* crowd out the traditional candy bar. They are so delicious; you will wonder why you ever put up with the sugar blues that the candies gave you.

In Appendix 6 you'll find the *Daniel Challenge Replacement Journal*. (Like the *Connecting Your Dots* charts in Appendix 2, these have been adapted from The Hallelujah Diet by George Malkmus with Peter & Stowe Shockey.) This journal is another valuable tool that will make your transition do-able and fun.

Empower Your Purpose: The Daniel FEAST! - Lesson Three

Scripture to Remember:

"As His anointing teaches you about all things…remain in Him."
1 John 2:27 (NIV)

Assignment #1: Look at your finances and see how much money is available for food, doctor co-pays, medicine, entertainment, and gifts. Next, make note of how much time is available for sick leave, or how much you can afford to be off work caring for family members. Now,  **connect the dots** between this information (about your resources and your present lifestyle) to see the potential success or devastation that may result if adjustments are not considered and acted upon. Are your spending habits taking you up or down? Ask God for insight as to how you could restructure and customize your finances and lifestyle to accommodate a health-building lifestyle. Consider the following: 1) food as your best medicine, 2) putting a stronger emphasis on the health of your body than the size (and expense) of your house, 3) using service to others as entertainment or creative (and free) entertainment, 4) cooperative stewardship of resources (i.e. a boat or cabin) with extended family or friends, 5) consolidating households among the generations, etc. (Appendix 7 is a budgeting worksheet for your convenience.)

Assignment #2: Read Appendix 8 on "Cravings" and be prepared for discussion.

Start NOW! Add raw nuts, seeds and avocado to your diet. A dehydrator that will adjust to 105 degrees is not a common item in our culture, but if you have one, soak the nuts according to the chart in Appendix 9, and then dry them until they are crispy. If you don't have access to a dehydrator, still add the nuts and seeds, but replace roasted and salted ones with raw ones. These are the good fats that our bodies need. A dehydrator can go on your wish list for the time you are ready to make this lifestyle adjustment.

" ... test us ... see how we look compared to the other young men who are eating the king's food. Then make your decision in light of what you see."

Lesson 4 – HOW-TOs

The Set Up and the Process for the Daniel FEAST

With five sons, a 242-acre ranch, bikes, a trampoline, horses, three fishing ponds, 200 pecan trees, an orchard, a crystal-clear ice-cold creek, and a garage that looked like a sporting goods store, we attracted many different families to our country home. Many hours were spent together in fellowship with friends in this comfortable place. More often than not, our friends' children stayed the night after their parents returned to Tulsa. One such family was the Buford family. Why am I bringing them up? Zachary. When I asked him what he would like for lunch he asked, "Do you have a veggie sandwich? I like mine with alfalfa sprouts, avocado, red onion, tomato and cucumber on whole grain toast, please." What happened to PBJ, chips and ice cream? When his mother picked him up, I asked about this mentality in her junior age son.

Zachary's mother shared with me about the health-building journey they were on with their doctor and personal friend, Dr. Joel Robbins. Dr. Robbins made educational opportunities available to his patients so that they could learn health-building principles and connect with others who were attempting to apply these truths to their own lives. Young Zachary and his family inspired me to keep moving forward in my attempts to learn and apply health-building skills. The more I learned, the more I realized that I wanted to use a positive approach with my family. If this family could do it, if young Zachary was willing to adapt to this DANIEL lifestyle of fresh, whole foods, my sons could, too. **I wanted to focus on adding all the wonderful foods that we had** *been missing out on, rather than creating a sense of injustice with my sons if I told them they couldn't have certain foods. I wanted to crowd out the harmful foods with the good foods. I wanted my sons to mature in their understanding of why we do what we do and connect the dots of cause and effect.*

Hopefully you have begun to **connect the dots** resulting in adjustments to your own life –whether in restructuring finances (homework assignment for Lesson 3) or beginning to consume living foods (homework assignment for this week's lesson). Have you noticed an increased desire to build a healthy lifestyle and to be around people who desire the same? I sure hope so! Then, how can you get others to come on board, specifically those in your own family?

Establish Your Support System:
Keys to Getting Your Family on Board

Let's talk about your family. These are the ones with whom your Creator strategically placed you. However, if you aren't geographically close to your biological family, or the ones that do live close aren't interested at this time, create a "family of necessity." Ask God to draw you together with others who desire this lifestyle. Is there a group of friends, maybe even through your church, who are meeting together on a weekly basis and "doing life" together? Start there! (Remember our role model, Daniel? His family was far away, yet he made it happen.)

> Building health is great fun and can/should be a family affair! It creates synergy and is much more do-able and fun **together!**

First: Educate your family about the benefits.

Consider the **family budget**, for example. (Most men respond well to this point). Is it *really* more expensive to eat wholesome meals and snacks? When our bodies are healthy, less money goes toward medications and doctors; and there is little income loss from missing work. Thus, there are more financial resources for ministry trips, helping the poor, upgrading the home and car (which will, in turn, empower your ministries more).

Compare the costs of chips, a candy bar, and pop versus the cost of a healthy meal. What is the difference? With the nutrient-robbing foods, the body needs *more food* because those types of foods only take away the hunger pangs *temporarily*. The body then asks for more 'usable' food to meet the nutritional needs and to make up for the nutrients lost when the body has to "pay the trash collector" (so to speak) to rid itself of the nutrient robbers.

When you compare the nutrient-dense foods to the nutrient-robbing foods, less food is needed because it is nutrient packed and meets more of the body's needs. The body is satisfied and doesn't ask for more. Neither do these foods harm your health later (creating the financial need for expensive medical treatment), but rather, they give you health!

> With health care costs so expensive, paying for the needs of our body is cheaper at the grocery store!

Initially it may cost more since the body is accustomed to more volume, and the foods consumed were nutrient-robbing foods, leaving the body wanting more. Once nutrient-dense foods are familiar to the body, it wants less, reducing your budget. You will need to plan financially for this "adjustment stage" in your household budget. Also, once you have fully adopted this new lifestyle, gained more information, made strong connections with health-building groups and have enjoyed some results, you will grow in confidence.

Families often rework their budgets to replace major medical health insurance, drug fees, and managing sick-leave days with the purchases of an accident policy, a catastrophic illness policy or an increase in vacations. You can't control all the variables in life; however, you can address many of them through this new lifestyle. One cost outweighs another, and the financial picture of the home tends to look better and better.

If you are still concerned about the amount of money needed to transition into a more health-building diet, consider the following story: *When I was 34 years old, my life took an unexpected turn. I became a single parent with less than one dollar to my name, an incomplete education and five sons to help to adulthood. People were so kind and generous to help me, some by randomly leaving food at my door. However, most of it was white (as opposed to whole grain), processed, canned and sugar laden. I prayed and asked God what to do about it since I already knew quite a bit about building health. The next day I found on my front porch sacks of produce, honey, and whole-wheat flour! Then, a friend of a friend called and said she had arranged for her father to go in to work - on his day off - and facilitate getting some emergency food stamps for us and to help me sign up for Aid to Families with Dependent Children. I had never even thought about receiving government help, but my extended family was unable to help me, and this door opened without my pursuing it.*

Later on, I was able to get my undergraduate degree in Family Studies and Gerontology. After I was no longer receiving government assistance, a generous benefactor paid for my Naturopathic Doctorate program! So you see, I find it difficult to believe that anyone with a heart for building health cannot do it. If you sincerely desire to make these changes, it is possible. Jehovah Jireh will make a way where there seems to be no way. Ask Him!

Actually, good health helps everyone around us. We'll continue to use the life of our role model, Daniel, in this illustration. As you recall, he faced a lions' den at one point in his life. When you don't give the body the things it needs to have good health, it may face the "lion" of sickness (disease). When you don't have energy or clear thinking to apply good relationship skills with family and friends, you may face a "lion" that divides your home (divorce). If the home divides, you may face a "lion" of lack (poverty). When stress increases due to all these unwanted changes, your personal style under stress may manifest in a harmful way you never dreamed you would act out (violence). When you are hurting while others around you have all they need, oftentimes the "lion" of poor choices comes around (crime). But the *DANIEL & Company* lifestyle can defeat those "lions" and help you and your loved ones put them under your feet as nothing more than lion-skin *rugs*!

Second: Pray for opportunities to plant seeds that will help your family connect the dots of symptoms with their food choices.

Remember that what you **don't know can hurt you!** Symptoms are not the enemy; they are your friends to help you know which foods (nutrients) are missing from your diet. Remember that **processed foods cannot give life** and they rob the body of stored nutrients which then cause symptoms. Therefore, we  simply **must connect the dots** between what we eat and our symptoms, as well as eating good food to reverse damage done by poor diet. We must focus on the benefits of healthy bodies, healthy families, healthy support groups, and healthy communities. (Later in this chapter I give an example of wording I used with my family when introducing this lifestyle.)

*"Do not be deceived, God cannot be mocked.
A man reaps what he sows."* Galatians 6:7 (NIV)

Third: Most everyone can relate to a desire for energy and a beautiful appearance.

Those who are healthy exhibit vibrancy and joy! These things are beautiful if you are a beauty contestant, a businessman or a stay-at-home mom. Consider this: Would you rather have hair that is falling out, blemished skin, dull eyes, and a bruised body ... or healthy looking skin, shiny hair, bright eyes, and a body filled with energy? The solution, as you know, is simple. The choice is yours!

Fourth: Take a positive approach.

A positive approach is the best way to connect with your family or "family of necessity". This is **huge**! There's so much more energy in the positive than in the negative.

| Use a Positive Focus - "Adding To" not "Taking Away From" |

First and most importantly, it's imperative to **focus on adding to**, not taking away from. If you were to say to yourself, "Don't think about the pink polka dot elephant," what would you think about? If you were to say, "Don't have candy, pastries, and soft drinks," what would you probably be thinking about?

If you refuse to take the <u>negative</u> approach of "no-no" and take a positive approach of "yes-yes; I **get** to have all these things I have been missing out on," then you will end up **crowding out** (with good food) what is *harming* you, and you will find that your body craves the nutrient-packed foods more than nutrient-draining foods. As you renew your mind with these thoughts and actions, you will experience your **tastes changing**, and you will find yourself wanting the <u>best</u> foods!

Fifth: Recognize the time commitment.

It's simple! Revolve your schedule around your body's needs OR you may be forced to revolve your schedule around your illness in the future. You will use your time and pay the price one way or another; it's your choice! I, for one, would rather spend time in my comfortable home, listening to beautiful music and preparing a wonderful snack, meal, or dehydrating some foods rather than spending hours in waiting rooms, pharmacies, admitting offices, or on hold with managed care helpers. Food and fellowship are so much more fun than medications, needles, procedures, or surgeries.

Start slowly and work into it, or go "cold turkey", whichever seems like the best approach for your circumstance. In lesson 5, we'll learn about the *Miracle in Wisconsin*. Theirs is a powerful story of how going "cold turkey" worked for Appleton Alternative School. Our family's story was more the "start slow and work into it approach." I had a strong focus on health even before I was married; however, I developed a more serious commitment as different needs arose and the opportunities to learn came along. The biggest changes in our lives came when several of my sons were still at home. Thus, at a family meeting I brought up the subject like this:

> Take a positive approach of "yes-yes; I **get** to have all these things I have been missing out on." then you will end up **crowding out** (with good food) what is *harming* you.

> "Guys, is now a good time to talk about something I'd like to do as a family? ... Good. The doors have opened for me to further my education. I have enrolled in a Naturopathic Doctorate program. I want to apply what I am learning here at home. I was wondering how you would feel about taking one night a week to test the ideas I will be learning. ... If we like it, we can do more. I will always have something on the table that

I know you like to make sure you don't leave the table hungry. I'd like for everyone to come focusing on how good this lifestyle will make you feel and how it will help us as a family. If we prepare ourselves with an open mind, one that is appreciative of all the new and wonderful things there are to add to our life, we'll be excited and willing to participate. Game? ... Great! We'll start this Thursday."

Well, our story has an awesome ending. It worked so well for us that we added Tuesdays to our Thursday health-building cuisine. We graduated into five days a week, and I provided all the junk they wanted on weekends. The result? We were so sluggish on Monday that they asked if I would keep the good foods all the time and minimize the junk foods. Now, we even have health-building *holidays.* Since then, we have added five daughters-in-law and fourteen grandchildren (and counting), as well as my husband, to our growing family. They all love the way they feel after eating the nutrient-dense foods. Even the grandchildren drink carrot juice and green drinks!

> In Appendix 10, look for some great tips that have proven successful in helping the most skeptical husbands and finicky or reluctant eaters to join in the fun.

Where do we start?
Set Up Your Kitchen

Your kitchen can be as simple and inexpensive (or extravagant) as you desire.

Here is a checklist of helpful kitchen items:
- ☐ Blender (most people already have one)
- ☐ Dish Soap

- [ ] Cutting Board (Vegetable/Fruit)
- [ ] A Second Cutting Board for Meat (to prevent cross contamination.)
- [ ] Hand Soap
- [ ] Juicer (Vegetable/Fruit)
  NOTE: We've tried many kinds and have two for different purposes. *The Juiceman Juicer* is the one my husband uses every morning. It is easy to use and easy to clean. We use the *Green Star Juicer* when we have less time for juicing. We can make this ahead, and it will retain a high portion of its nutrition because it pulverizes rather than using centrifugal force.
- [ ] Citrus Juicer (For one or two lemons in recipes. I prefer my glass one rather than the electric type.)
- [ ] Pint-Sized Canning Jars with Lids (These will work with many blenders. Screwed onto the base of the blender it works like a bullet blender using the blender you already have to make individual servings for on-the-go. These can also be used with the *Green Star* juicer to make some juices ahead of time.)
- [ ] Plastic Butcher Knife (Metal tends to turn the produce brown faster. Use this when cutting off the base of Romaine lettuce and celery before washing.)
- [ ] Salad Shooter (This is a great tool to help finicky eaters by making the new veggies very small when adding them to the salad. It also adds beautiful color. Remember, colors represent different vitamins. A variety of them are needed.)
- [ ] Salad Spinner
- [ ] Sanitation Disinfectant by Sink
- [ ] Stainless Steel Bake Ware
- [ ] Stainless Steel Cookware
- [ ] Steaming Tray or Vegetable/Rice Steamer
- [ ] Strainer (Over the Sink)
- [ ] Strainer (Small Round)
- [ ] Vegetable Brush
- [ ] Vinegar
- [ ] Water Purifier

*Some of these items won't be necessary once you make a complete transition.

Shopping

Since our goal in this lesson for *The Daniel Lifestyle* (*Daniel Fast or Daniel Diet*, if that is how you are using it) is to help people who are primarily eating processed foods add a variety of fresh, raw, bright, living, nutrient-dense, health-building foods to their diet, then shopping for those foods is very easy. Go back to Lesson 3 and look at the foods you highlighted (the ones you already like) and put them on your grocery list. Then, pick out a few more that you would be willing to try. In our city we have a store that matches prices, so we incorporate the sale items into our weekly menu.

Depending upon the season of the year, go to your local farmer's market to purchase produce. Local farmers typically leave fruits and vegetables on the plant or tree longer, which retains more nutrition and flavor. If it's the off-season and your farmer's markets are closed, and you are able to shop the organic food stores, do so as they are better for you and typically taste better due to the lack of chemicals. However, if you can't afford them at this time, then do the best you can with what you have. Pray and trust Jehovah Jireh to open doors for you financially so you can transition to more health-building levels.

Appendix 11 is a list of the *Dirty Dozen and Clean Fifteen*, which are the produce with the most and least herbicide or pesticide contamination. If you can't totally shop organic, purchase as much as you can according to this list, as well as dried fruits since during the drying process any chemicals that are on the produce will be concentrated. Remember: Just because you are shopping in a health food store does not mean you are getting all organic. As a matter of fact, I have found that when the health food store can't get organic, they will provide conventional. Please note that this is for your convenience and, like purchasing milk at a gas station, it will cost more. I have found it to be consistently a dollar a pound higher where I live and shop.

Ten times better!

Teamwork and Your Support System

Here are a few tips to get you and your "family" to make this lifestyle do-able and fun.

> ➤ **Shop together** (teach by example and lighten the load on the main grocery shopper). Depending upon their ages, send the kids to get specific items within the store.

> ➤ **Delegate** items to family members for pickup who have the means of transport. If your support team consists of all adults who drive, then divide up the shopping by geographic area and have one person pick up health food store items, another pick up traditional store items, sale items, co-op items, water store items, etc.

> ➤ **Call** when you finish checking out at the store and inform those at home that you are on your way so they can be available to help carry in, wash, prepare, put away.

> ➤ **Clean the kitchen before leaving for the store** or delegate the responsibility to someone while you are gone shopping. (All sinks, strainers, and the refrigerator need to be clean and sanitized).

Preparing the Produce for "Good Food Fast"

> For those who would like additional visuals to learn how to prepare your produce, visit our website (www.MAKINGthyme.com) to access a helpful power point.

There are many thoughts on the best way to clean your produce. They range greatly in cost and time commitment. Two very effective (and expensive ways) to kill gnat and fruit fly eggs and germs can be found at www.enagic.com (Kangen water machines) and www.sunrider.com (SunSmile Fruit and Vegetable Rinse). Now for a couple of less expensive ways to do the job. The Hallelujah Diet® teaches to fill two spray bottles – one with distilled vinegar and another with hydrogen peroxide. Spray the produce first with vinegar, followed immediately with the hydrogen peroxide. Let stand three to five minutes, and then rinse. A second less expensive way to clean produce is with vinegar and water. Although there doesn't seem to be agreement on the amount of vinegar to use with filtered water, there is complete agreement that vinegar and water can remove 98% germs found on the food, as well as kill the gnat and fruit fly eggs. Therefore, fill your sinks with cold filtered water. Then add apple cider vinegar according to your research. We use enough so that it's easy to tell that the vinegar is in there, but not enough to smell like a pickle factory.

Sink load #1 - your **cleanest produce first**, such as apples, grapes, strawberries, blueberries, blackberries, bananas, oranges, peppers, squashes, etc. Leave them for a few minutes while you spread out dishcloths on the counter and put your strainers on top of them. Remove produce from vinegar water, rinse with water and place in strainers. The water is still fine to add another sink full of produce.

Sink load #2 - lettuce, kale, celery, watermelon, cantaloupe, muskmelon; they are typically dirtier and can go in this batch. (Cut off the base of the lettuce and celery before placing it in the water.) Run your hands over the produce, loosening any dirt that may not have yet come off. The dirt will settle to the bottom of the sink. When you pull these items out, keep like items together and place the leafy type into a **salad spinner**. Spin them a few times, stopping to pour off excess water between each spin. Put them in **plastic bags** with a couple of **white paper towels.** "**Vacuum pack**" them by putting the bag in between your body and the cabinet and gently leaning on it, securing the top as the air comes out.

Sink load #3 - root vegetables such as beets and radishes. These make the water the dirtiest. You may want to use a **vegetable brush** on these. Be sure to place the beets on a dark towel, as they will stain things a bright red color. Put these items in a plastic bag with paper towels. When washing potatoes, wash them in a **sink of their own with fresh water.** After gently scrubbing, place them on towels to air dry. Then put them with the garlic and onion in a **covered basket** so dust won't settle on them.

Arrange everything else in your refrigerator according to use. In my refrigerator, the **juicing items** go on the side closest to the way the refrigerator opens. The 15-pound bag of carrots is on the bottom shelf; the strainer of apples and lemons is on the shelf above. The kale and beet tops are in the drawer underneath the carrots. (By the way, we don't wash the carrots until right before we juice. We buy in such bulk that we feel it keeps them from going bad if we wait to wash them.) Note how the produce is grouped in strainers for specific purposes, i.e. salsa, guacamole, juicing, salads, snacks, etc.

Empower Your Purpose: The Daniel FEAST! - Lesson Four

The **snack type foods** are placed in separate strainers or kept stored in their containers from the store. The two or three different kinds of grapes are cut into palm sized bunches and arranged beautifully in a round strainer. The top of the strawberry container is trimmed off to make easy access; otherwise, they tend to go bad before they are eaten. (And yes, I did put the entire container unopened into the water; likewise on blueberries, blackberries and raspberries.) Don't trim off the green leafy strawberry top. Use it for a "handle" when snacking. Also, it is prettier with the green top when used as an edible garnish.

All the **citrus** (oranges, limes, Clementine oranges, pineapple) go into a strainer or bowl together making a visual delight for the eyes. We put all the ingredients for **guacamole** or **mango salsa** in the same strainer or bowl so it's real easy and fast when time to make it. Everything for **salads** goes into the other crisper. We do not precut anything, because oxidation begins when we open the skin seal of the produce. It takes no time at all to whip up any kind of salad once all the produce is clean and organized in the refrigerator.

We also put together the items that we often lightly **steam**; these would include all the squashes, green beans and new or fingerling potatoes.

We typically purchase 30 to 35 different fruits and vegetables a week and rotate those to include the less popular ones, such as fresh coconuts, pomegranates, plums, nectarines, etc.

Also purchase raw nuts, olive oil, olives (you can start with canned if you like), whole grain wraps, whole grain or gluten free breads and crackers, brown rice, oatmeal, and others. Look at your list in Lesson 3 and experiment with different pantry foods.

Great job! You have begun a journey that will **connect the dots** for a healthy future, not just for you but also for your family and generations to come. All this talk about food has made me hungry. Time for a snack? Yes, I believe so!

Ten times better!

Scripture to Remember:

"All things are lawful for me, but not all things are profitable. All things are lawful for me, but I will not be mastered by anything." 1 Corinthians 6:12 (NASB)

Assignment: Think about examples of people you know whom you believe have relational issues based on their mood swings, energy levels, health problems, etc. Think of examples of times you felt more motivated to seek the Lord and do His will and times that you just weren't interested. Did illness or lack of energy play into these examples? Do you understand the importance of food in our spiritual and natural relationships?

Start NOW! Add baked or grilled chicken and fish to your diet and limit your red meat consumption to special occasions, and then have it as seasoning (like in stir fry) rather than as a huge portion. See meats, especially red meat, as transitional foods. For maximum productivity and vibrant health, nutrient dense and easily digested foods are found in a plant-based diet such as Daniel's.

*" ... test us ... see how we look compared to the other young men
who are eating the king's food.
Then make your decision in light of what you see."*

Lesson 5 – SYNERGY

*Your Lifestyle on Course with Your Creator, Family
& Friends*

"Tag, you're it." One of the pastor's six sons ran by and punched me in the shoulder. "It" again. Before deciding whom I would chase to pass on my title, I ran over the small bridge which crossed the creek to the picnic area. There the mound of fried fish and hushpuppies with green onions was growing by the minute. My daddy was feeding the entire church with this fish fry. Along with the fish was his delicious recipe of coleslaw and cold, sliced tomatoes freshly picked from the garden. Momma was there too, arranging the tables, centerpieces, napkins and silverware to make it feel special. She was pouring her love into the environment with the same energy that Daddy was by making the food appealing. "We eat with our eyes, Betsy Jane," he would say to me. "Make it as beautiful to look at as it is delicious to eat."

With an at-home mother and a father in his retirement season, hospitality in our home was the norm. If it wasn't the church we were feeding, it was the latest missionary or revival speaker visiting the small community. Fellowship around the table, and the diverse stories and cultures that accompanied them, enriched my young life. It did more than enrich it; it helped define it. This connecting with people around food, fun, and learning is **who I am**. These activities – food, fun, fellowship - are **what I am to do with my life** and **give me direction as to where I am to go**. These people are **the ones with whom I am to go through life**.

This connection, centered around food, carried over into my adult life as I enlarged my circle of friends. It wasn't unusual to get a phone call like this: "Betsy, this is Sherry ... What are you having for supper tonight? ... Stir-fry and rice? ... I'll bring homemade egg rolls ... See you at 5:00 ... Bye!" No words of "Could we come over," just "I'll bring..." We had that kind of relationship. I LOVED it! It wasn't just Chuck, Sherry, and Sarah. Monday night homemade-pizza-salad-and-cinnamon-rolls-night with the Sawyers took place for years. We learned so much about life from "doing life" with the diverse group of friends that Divine providence brought into our lives, and us into theirs. Living life with a focus on building physical and relational health was definitely a process. We weren't doing all the health-building things perfectly. **We were learning and growing together.** *Step by step.*

As you will find out, learning and growing (no matter how slow the progression may be) is part of the process. And when we can do so with others, especially those we love and enjoy, it makes the journey so much more fun! In the introduction to this course, you learned my motive for putting these materials together: to see disease and divorce eradicated. Thus, physical and relational health is my passion. We briefly touched on the effect good health has on relational and societal components of our lives (Lesson 3). However, up to this point, we have primarily focused on the <u>physical</u> component. In this chapter we are going to shift into a stronger focus on the <u>relational</u> aspect. Why? To answer that question, let's view a few images that portray the importance of "the group", i.e. "family."

Consider ... Why do birds fly in this pattern? Why do they not fly alone?

Now, look at the picture of this elephant herd. All the baby elephants are in the center of the ring, and all the adult elephants surround them with their tusks facing out to fight off the enemy and protect the young.

Empower Your Purpose: The Daniel FEAST! - Lesson Five

Take a moment to read Ephesians 6:12 and John 10:10. According to these verses, we are in a battle against a real enemy - an enemy that wants to steal, kill and destroy. He is crafty and won't tempt us with something that won't entice us, but will "coat the poison" so we don't realize the harm it is causing.  **We need each other** to help identify the enemy, and also to help us mature in our thinking so that we may gain victory over the behaviors which are killing us.

> It is much easier to eat healthy when it's the norm of your community, i.e. like flying in a 'V'.

First Corinthians 12 teaches us that we were created like a puzzle piece; with parts to contribute to others and a need to receive the part others have to give. We are social beings. That teaching is **counter-cultural** from the **rugged American individualistic attitude** of the society in which we live. But let me relieve some guilt and insecurity by emphatically stating, *You were not meant to do life alone; to carry all the responsibilities of home, work, family and community without intergenerational and extended family help; nor to defeat the evil one by yourself!* Relationships are not just important; they are absolutely necessary! In a country where families often survive financially without help from extended family, the stress of doing life without a strong family support team is having a noticeable effect.

For **last week's homework** you were to think about examples of people you know whom you believe have relational issues based on their mood swings, energy levels, or health problems. You were to think about times you felt more motivated to seek the Lord and do His will and times that you just weren't interested. You were asked if illness or lack of energy play into these examples. Now do you see a correlation between a healthy lifestyle and healthy spiritual and natural relationships?

Can you **connect the dots** in the following sentences? An unhealthy lifestyle will render symptoms of physical and relational illness. These illnesses are revealed in the use of medications and surgeries to alleviate pain and dysfunction. These illnesses result in lost wages, debt and lost opportunities to advance or contribute to important causes. These illnesses can change our focus from helping others to  merely surviving. Oftentimes divorce and poverty result, and sometimes **violence** and **crime** follow. Who would have thought food would play such an important part in the well being of our families and in the safety of our communities?

Crumbling Families

I chose the following study because it was released during the time I had a houseful of children at home, and is still being used today. (Does that tell us that statistics are not revealing improvement?) This study from the U.S. Census Bureau ("Children's Well-Being: An International Comparison," U.S. Department of Commerce, Bureau of the Census, November, 1990 and digitized in 2009), compares the United States with other developed countries, and presents alarming evidence of family and relational fragmentation. Since the 1980s our country has had:

- The highest divorce rate in the world (64% higher than any other country studied).
- The highest percentage of children raised by a single parent.
- The highest teen pregnancy rate in the world.
- The highest percentage of violent deaths among youth.
- A homicide rate that is five times higher than that of any other developed country, except Mexico.

There have also been increases in the number of families suffering from the effects of depression, alcoholism, physical or sexual abuse – with a wide range of other serious relational problems.

> You were not meant to do life alone; carry all the responsibilities of home, work, family and community without intergenerational and extended family help; nor defeat the evil one by yourself!

Do you see a progression from the breakdown of the family to safety in our communities? We said earlier, "What we don't know can KILL us." (From these statistics, it looks like that is true in more ways than one!)

In his book *Two Dates or Less*, Neil Clark Warren, a noted marriage and family specialist and creator of *eHarmony* said that, "Failed marriages and family breakdown are significant causes of the **social chaos, violence** and **turmoil** around the world." He also stated, "If we can *reduce the divorce rate* in the United States by *just 5 percent*, this will affect more than one million people in a generation (not to mention the millions in the following generations)." He continued, "Even more exciting: 'If we can reduce the divorce rate in our country to single digits, it will represent **the most important social revolution in the history of the world.**'"

How Our Lifestyle Affects Our Responsibilities

In the 1950s, stay-at-home-moms were seen as essential to the family structure (think June Cleaver here). Nurture and nutrition of the family were priorities. Houses became "homes" as parents loved their children and gave them and their needs top priority. The time and energy put into the home translated as value and love to its inhabitants. Today we seem to have shifted to the she-can-do-it-all-super-woman mentality. Dr. James Dobson had a strong opinion about what that was doing to today's young women, didn't he? (See Appendix 3.) I'll add to that the need to consider the following:

Businesses hire cleaning services, food services, and child care services, but a woman who works outside her home is expected to take care of all of those services in addition to her full-time job, often working overtime as well. What quality of services can be expected when this is the case? Is there a correlation between health of the family, marital satisfaction, the divorce rate, the anger of today's youth and our lifestyles, roles, diet...?

Titus 2 gives a strong mandate for the older women to teach the younger women priorities in the home and with their own families. Proverbs 31 provides an example of a woman who is multi-talented and has a significant budget to pay additional helpers. I'm not advocating that mothers should never work outside the home. I <u>am</u> advocating that **the children and home should not be neglected** for a higher standard of living. There are so many things that money cannot buy, but they are felt for a lifetime if neglected. The nurture of biological parents is one of them.

> It is important to acknowledge the connection between food, purpose, relationships, exercise, hygiene, rest and health in order to function (as closely as possible) according to the Creator's design.

How Our Lifestyle Affects Our Relationships

Not only do poor eating habits affect our physical health, but our emotional health as well. Poor food choices lead to poor self-image, isolation, bad moods, irritability, uncontrolled anger, mental confusion, and depression (See page 63, <u>*The Amazing Connection between...Food and Love*</u> by Dr. Gary Smalley). If you are dealing with any of those symptoms, you can obtain relief through a simple lifestyle change.

In contrast, healthy food choices lead to strong self-image, connections, good moods, patience, controlled anger, clear thinking, and joy. Which characteristics would you rather have in your life?

THE POSITIVE CYCLE

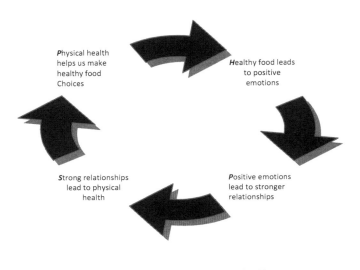

THE NEGATIVE CYCLE

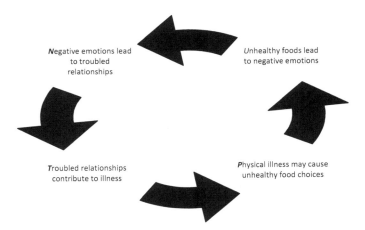

Ten times better!

The story about the *Miracle in Wisconsin* (written overview in Appendix 12; video available at www.MAKINGthyme.com) is a very powerful, present-day demonstration of the effect good nutrition can have on deviant behavior. If it can so greatly affect negative extremes in our society, think how it can enhance your family, work and school relationships!

Now that you, hopefully, realize the consequences of poor nutrition on relationships, families, communities, and the energy and clear thinking that are available with good nutrition, let us once again view the holistic approach in the life of Daniel. In Lesson 2 we stated that Daniel, much like Christ, knew who he was, where he was going, with whom he was going, and how to empower himself for his purpose. So now, I'd like to raise awareness of information that, when learned and assimilated into your life and the lives of your support system, can be used as an arsenal of power against division.

Jesus said, *"I know where I've come from and where I go next, You don't know where I'm from or where I'm headed."*
John 8:13-16 (MSG)

First of all, "Who are you?"

So often people focus on things they cannot change rather than focus on things that they can greatly influence through understanding, teaching, and development. A popular teacher in the 1970s through 1990s (Bill Gothard) defined "The Ten Unchangeables" as follow:

1. One of a Kind
2. Parents
3. Siblings
4. Nationality
5. Mental Capacity
6. Time in History
7. Gender

8. Birth Order
9. Aging (Genetics)
10. Death (Timing)

I have had the privilege of working with several ministries dedicated to helping people discover their identity and their purpose. Each one has different areas of expertise. Most, if not all of them, assess and teach the following topics:

1. Communication Style
2. Conflict Resolution Skills
3. Life Experiences
4. Ministry Gifts
5. Motivational Gifts
6. Personality
7. Passions
8. Personal Habits: Etiquette
9. Roles: Traditional or Non-traditional
10. Energizing Activities

Local churches are typically great resources for classes and assessments that may help you discover your strengths and increase your confidence. I encourage you to tap into these resources that will help you more fully develop the part you are to play in history, and to do it with your family!

These materials are highly recommended for further study:
• Gary Smalley – *Personality Tests*   • Bill Gothard – *Ten Unchangeables*   • John Trent – *Life Mapping*   • Fred & Florence Littauer – *Personality Profile*   • Don & Katie Fortune – *Discover Your God Given Gifts*   • Jane A.G. Kise, David Stark, Sandra Krebs Hirsh - *Life Keys*   • Neil Clark Warren – *Two Dates or Less*

- Marita Littauer – *Wired That Way*
- Rick Warren – *The Purpose Driven Life*
- Cynthia Tobias – *The Way They Learn*
- Keven Leman – *The Birth Order Book*
- Dave Jewitt – Your One Degree

Secondly, "Where are you going?"

What is your assignment in life? Many people are ashamed of or extremely frustrated by their biological family, even to the point that they reject them. They form a "family of election" where they decide with whom they will go through life. This problem has many facets, two of which I'd like to mention here:

#1. When we reject our biological family, we miss out on keys that can help us understand the "why" behind much of our behavior. You see, family systems have beliefs. Those beliefs motivate behavior. You can struggle a lifetime with a behavior that, were you looking into the mirror of your parents, siblings, aunts, uncles and cousins, you could see the belief that drives the behavior and disable it more quickly.

#2. When we reject our family of origin, we neglect our responsibility to care for them. In the bigger picture of social order and a life of meaning and satisfaction, family units provide the structure most effective in meeting needs. You see, at one point or another, everyone will face burdens bigger than they can handle on their own. Help will be needed. When the family is functioning well, the need can be met quickly. When family can't meet the need, the Bible states that the church is to help with those needs. In our society, the government has stepped up to the plate to meet needs that were designed for a smaller unit; thus, it caters to the masses rather than customizing to the individual or family need. That creates waste, abuses, loss of dignity, and unnecessary stresses and frustration. It can also promote **crime** and **violence**. "Some years ago, the late British historian, Arnold Toynbee, spent some time in the United States. Upon leaving this country he observed that of all the places in which to be poor, America was the worst because of its vast wealth. To be poor when everyone around you is similarly afflicted is hard, but to be poor when most are comfortable and many are rich can be unbearable!"

I realize that there are those whose parents (and sometimes whole families) are no longer living. However, these are in the minority. As we stated before, the Creator set up family systems as the basis for social order where customized care can be given more effectively. Granted, some families have much more to work with than others. To that statement I would respond, *From everyone who has been given much, much will be required* (Luke 12:48, NASB). If your family system is full of deviant behavior or addictions, realize this: **you can be the transitional generation**. You can be the one that brings new life to your family tree! Your deepest anointing may come out of your greatest challenge. For instance, if I overcame addiction to food, sexual addiction, drug addiction, or pharisaical beliefs and behaviors, I could be the "resident expert" in that particular challenge. Rather than it defining me in a negative way, it would become the way I can most effectively contribute to society.

> Your deepest anointing may come out of your greatest challenge.

Third, "With whom are you going?"

Once we have recognized *who we are* apart from *what we do* and have accepted our "assignment" (identified through our family system), then we will be more effective in identifying whom we need to recognize as ideal marriage partners and those with whom we must form additional ministry or business teams. Some effective questions from Neil Clark Warren to help determine this are as follows:

- Do his or her dreams overlap with your dreams?
- Does he or she have/not have your "Must Haves" / "Can't Stands"?
- Does he or she value your qualities?

- Does he or she "sparkle" when you are together?
- Are our "Crucial Similarities" intact?
    1. Spiritual harmony
    2. Desire for verbal intimacy
    3. Ability to be intimate
    4. Energy level
    5. Level of ambition
    6. Expectations about roles
    7. Interests
    8. Personal habits

"Make a careful exploration of who you are and what you have been given, and then sink yourself into that. Don't be impressed with yourself. Don't compare yourself with others. Each of you must take responsibility for doing the creative best you can with your own life."
Galatians 6:4-5 (MSG)

Each of us is like a puzzle piece. We have *strengths* (something to give), *growth areas* (our road to maturity in our strengths), and *gaps* (areas where we have nothing to give that need to be filled by healthy relationships). When our growth areas are noted (after we validate the strengths of who we are), hope arises. So often people frame growth areas as weaknesses, and that causes frustration and rejection. Positively accepting others with their growth areas is so much more powerful than negating or shunning people because of their weaknesses. If a  **paradigm shift** resulting in the positive terms *strengths, growth areas,* and *gaps* were used (instead of the negative term of weaknesses), people could choose to focus on the fact, in the words of Rocky to Adrian: "You got gaps. I got gaps. Together, we ain't got no gaps!"

Empower Your Purpose: The Daniel FEAST! - Lesson Five

Scripture to Remember:

"... so our body would not be divided. God wanted the different parts to care the same for each other. If one part of the body suffers, all the other parts suffer with it. Or if one part of our body is honored, all the other parts share its honor."
1 Corinthians 12:25-26 (NCV)

Assignment:

- Ask your Creator to guide you in designing do-able and fun steps for implementing the information you have received to build your physical and relational health naturally. Come prepared to share the creative ideas the Holy Spirit has given you.
- Watch the *Miracle in Wisconsin* video online at www.MAKINGthyme.com
- Evaluate the effectiveness of your family's ability to affirm diversity and build confidence in each of its members, resolve conflict in a healthy way, discover and validate and empower each person's individual calling, and seek to understand how that calling fits  together with the family system. Watch for opportunities the Lord provides for gaining additional insight, understanding and skills. After considering the good plans your Creator has for you, we invite you to pray the prayers in Appendix 13 to invite His guidance and power in your life for a health building lifestyle. **And if you have never started your spiritual journey with Jesus Christ as your Savior, there is some guidance and a suggested prayer there to help you as well.**

Start NOW! In the following lesson, you will take a look at the **DANIEL CHALLENGE**. Setting up a lifestyle makeover team will double the fun as you transition into the **good** life!

> *" ... test us ... see how we look compared to the other young men who are eating the king's food. Then make your decision in light of what you see."*

Lesson 6 – GAME-ON

Four Levels of the DANIEL CHALLENGE

"Okay, guys, it's ready," I called as I dumped the last load of laundry on top of the pile that was now taller than the toddler standing there watching with blanket in one hand and thumb in his mouth. Little towheaded boys came running from every direction. The oldest would fold t-shirts, #2 would fold the jeans, #3 got the bath towels, #4's job was underwear stacking, and the baby got to pick out socks. "On your mark, get set, GO!" And in short order the mound of laundry disappeared. Now for the real fun. Socks were made into sock balls and the laundry baskets opposing one another created the "court", and phase two of the "housework" began. Living on a large ranch with a household of wee ones and a plethora of company, there was always much work to be done. Creative juices flowed, and ideas for making work "fun" flowed as needed. Competition or games made folding clothes, mowing acres, clearing fence row, picking pecans or caring for the animals that much more fun. Why? It was relational. And it didn't stop in our family with that generation. Although the ranch has been sold to another intergenerational family (also with five children born within 7 years), "Happy Drinks" and other enjoyable family traditions continue the legacy of making life fun. **Anything that creates good memories and makes life enjoyable for all can facilitate change in a do-able, meaningful, and satisfying way.**

Is there really a way to make this a journey filled with fun ... that lasts? I trust that, in this final lesson together, we will **connect the dots** between how we get from where we are to where we want to be and

need to be. How can we transition from filling our bodies with nutrient-robbing foods to nutrient-dense foods? How can all these changes be made without feeling like we are missing out? More than that, how can it all be done so that everyone on the journey really enjoys the "ride"?

> *"... there were 200 leaders...with their relatives... all men who understood the temper of the times and knew the BEST COURSE...to take."*
> I Chronicles 12:32 (TLB)

Growth Analysis

Becoming healthy is a growth process. Where are you in your journey to healthy living? Take a look at the list below. Most people begin to add the items at the beginning of the list and work their way down. However, feel free to make the changes that work best for you and your family first. Then take on the more challenging ones later.

- ☐ Fresh fruits
- ☐ Fresh salad
- ☐ Raw nuts & seeds
- ☐ Legumes
- ☐ Healthy fats
  (Start with avocado and nuts, but pure raw oils such as olive and grapeseed are fine too.)
- ☐ Purified water
- ☐ Freshly made juice
- ☐ Baked fish
- ☐ Baked chicken
- ☐ Organics
- ☐ Locally grown
- ☐ 70-80% natural or raw food

Ten times better!

- ☐ 20-30% social/not as healthy foods / transitional foods for a transitional generation
(Grow into making these vegan or vegetarian choices, and then a smaller and smaller percentage of cooked foods while increasing the raw foods for optimal health.)
- ☐ Whole food supplements
Are these made from organic, whole foods? Cold pressed?
- ☐ Chiropractic adjustments
- ☐ Dental cleanings

Many people gravitate towards a diet. This journey is not about a diet that you are on today and get off of later. This is about the Creator's design for your body and a lifestyle change. **It is important to acknowledge the connection between food, purpose, relationships, exercise, hygiene, rest and health in order to function (as closely as possible) according to the Creator's design.** Our primary focus in this study has been on the food and relational aspects; however, below are listed a few more important components to our **holistic** approach to health.

- Knowing who you are (your life's purpose)
- Knowing where you are going
- Knowing with whom you are going
- Knowing your need to rest, be still, and re-focus
- Exercising and time in nature (aside from the physical exertion of your occupation)
- Developing good hygiene (daily physical and spiritual cleansing)
- Choosing a nutrient-packed diet (as listed above)

Nutrition Analysis

I have found that **food has an emotional and relational connection**. To make the adjustment from health-robbing foods to health-building foods, **make note of what you eat and why you eat it**. Then, purpose to find healthier alternatives for those items. We can ask ourselves questions such as, "Am I eating this as an emotional connection to someone I love? Do I like the texture – creaminess, crunchiness? Do I like the taste – salty, sweet, sour, spicy? Why?" You see, our bodies are telling us something with each one of these answers, but oftentimes, in our lack of knowledge or understanding, we give our bodies harmful alternatives to what they are asking for. After studying how to build health, rather than fight disease, I would know that when I crave creaminess, I could possibly need good fats. When I crave salt, I may be dehydrated and my body is trying to keep in the liquid I presently have. Sweet cravings could be telling me that I need energy from fruits. Crunchy cravings could be saying, "Eat your veggies. You need minerals." If we crave things that we enjoyed with a loved one gone by, we may be needing to connect with another human being who is an important part of our assignment in life, helping us to fulfill our purpose.

For example, our family watched Walt Disney every Sunday evening when I was a little girl. We would gather in the living room around the TV. Daddy would pop the popcorn and put it into the various sized bowls. Momma would cut up the apples. It was a very sweet "together" time for our family. To this day, it's difficult to watch a movie or family show without the huge grocery bag of popcorn. (We had a large family - seven children - and it took a lot of popcorn!)

Also, my husband, who loves to jog and loves chocolate almond shakes, would promise himself one of those shakes as he pushed himself for extended distances.

Now, though, we have found healthier alternatives to these foods that have emotional and relational connections. For instance, instead of my husband's chocolate-almond-shake-motivate-me-to-finish-this-jog drink, we now make a delicious alternative that contains nut milks, coconut butter, agave or honey, carob and chopped almonds. This is a thick, creamy, health-building substitute. For my popcorn memory, I make an olive oil, garlic, sea salt, brewers yeast (cheesy) kale chip which is delicious! Or if I just *really* want popcorn, I use a healthier alternative by air-popping it, then putting the good-for-me oils and seasonings on it. Our symbolic holiday foods are made with fresh and raw ingredients that are nutrient dense rather than robbing, for the most part. The meat portions are cut into small-pieces (rather than a large slab) and eaten only at that special time of the year, not as a meat and potato every night dinner option. There are so many AMAZING foods available to which we have never been introduced due to the fast-food and traditional-foods we inherited when the last generations were blown off course.

Take a few minutes to analyze your lifestyle and dietary habits. Please know that these questions are not asked to bring about condemnation, but rather to allow you to take an honest look for the purpose of determining your starting place. In the chart below, record an example of what you typically eat.

	Best Day	Number per week	Worst day	Number per week
Breakfast				
Lunch				
Dinner				
Snacks				

What do you eat when you want comfort food?
_____
_____

What do you eat when you are entertaining or eating socially?
_____
_____

What do you eat when you need quick energy?
_____
_____

> There are terrific recipes in which to find similar replacements for the things you already love that are harming you. Pray for direction, use friends as good resources and search Google, too. Some great places to start:
> The Hallelujah Diet® 1 (855) 414.1331 (Toll-Free), www.thetwosisters.com, www.wholefoods.com, www.alissacohen.com, www.toprawmen.com, www.cleanseamerica.com
> The book *Raw Food Cleanse* is also excellent. It's author, Penni Shelton, was one of my first students. She took our teaching, her love of healthy foods, and created this resource of recipes.

Readiness for Change

How big is your commitment to change?
_____
_____

Can your life handle the abruptness of going cold turkey?
_____

What are your commitments?

_____
_____

- Family responsibilities (After the birth of the baby? Grandma is on hospice in your home?):

_____
_____

- Work outside the home (Just started a new job? Traveling and don't know how to do this on the road yet?):

_____
_____

How much time do you have to prepare foods?

☐ None
☐ Very little
☐ At least 30 minutes
☐ An hour or more

Do you have access to a food prep area at work?

☐ Yes
☐ No

What does your support system look like?

- In the home:

_____
_____

- Outside the home:

_____
_____
_____

What did your Budget Worksheet (Appendix 7) reveal about how you could reprioritize purchasing more living, organic foods? What steps can you take to begin this process?

_____
_____
_____

Customize Your Plan

Now that you have taken an honest look at the journey toward relational and physical health, does it all seem overwhelming? You, or someone you know, may have attempted a similar lifestyle change before and failed. Maybe you are tired of trying and not succeeding. As I've said throughout this study, this lifestyle change is do-able. What, then, is the key to success? Doing it with your Creator and others, and at the same time making it fun!

"[Not in your own strength] for it is God Who is all the while effectually at work in you [energizing and creating in you the power and desire], both to will and to work for His good pleasure and satisfaction and delight." Philippians 2:13 (AMP)

"Two are better than one, because they have a good return for their work: If one falls down, his friend can help him up." Ecclesiastes 4:9-10a (NIV)

One way to make this journey do-able and fun is to find a place where you can belong, can receive encouragement, and have an opportunity for growth. Remember the picture of the birds in their flying formation in Lesson 5? Let me encourage you to find *your* "V" – family members or a group of like-minded and like-spirited individuals that will provide consistent accountability, offer protection from the lies of the enemy by speaking the truths learned in these lessons, and encourage you to continue on your journey. We have created what we are calling "DANIEL CHALLENGES" as tools to help you and your "V" of loved ones apply these materials. Remember, that Daniel was so confident that this lifestyle was the best one that he asked the man overseeing he and his friends the following: "Please test us for ten days. See how we look compared to the other young men. Then make your decision in light of what you see." Let me walk you through the set-up process for our modern day "test".

1. Invite your family to participate. If there are not enough participants to create nice-sized teams - one vs. one isn't nearly as much fun or powerful as several vs. several - then invite your family of necessity or co-workers, etc. If you would like, pick a team name and team color.
2. Check out the **DANIEL CHALLENGES** below. There are categories for holistic health goals. Choose how many you will set as goals. Make it do-able for your situation. You can always participate in another **DANIEL CHALLENGE** (with a focus on more categories) at a more do-able time. (Your symptoms will always be there to remind you that we are here and you can join in. Don't condemn yourself if you need to start small. Just <u>starting</u> is a VICTORY!) Once you choose your goals, make it known to the group. You will be competing against yourself, but contributing to the victory of your team by meeting your customized goals. (For example, everyone doesn't have to lose 20 pounds. Your goal may be to just make fresh juice every morning ... period. However, just because there's no pressure to do it all, don't be lazy. If you are in a position to do more, do it! It's in your best interest! Besides, once you've done it long enough, it will become your habit and lifestyle ... and you get all the benefits!)

Suggestion: Set up a private FB page or free website just for your group where you can post words of encouragement and victory, or struggles, recipes, etc., as well as, your points. Download PDF files of your individual and team charts from our website.

There is a free iPhone app that tracks your running, biking, nutrition, then records it and also makes it available to share with others. Whether you are tech savvy enough to set this up for your group up or use the paper and pen style of recording it with the charts we provide, let me encourage you to do *something* to connect with others and apply this material.

DANIEL'S 1-Time "Acquire-A-Taste" CHALLENGE   (a.k.a. "Got Juice")

It's simple. You can't acquire a taste if you won't try it. This challenge is for people who will begin the process of acquiring a taste by trying our signature drink (carrot, lemon, apple). Your orange moustache will start you on a journey of great energy and health building.

DANIEL'S 10-Day "Add To" CHALLENGE

This challenge is for those who are willing to spend 10 days adding nutrient dense foods to their diet. It will help you discover a whole new world of nutrient-dense, energy foods. In this challenge you can continue to eat anything you typically eat. The only catch is that you must eat the nutrient-dense foods first for 10 days. The body's cut-off mechanism will be experienced, signaling that you've been properly fueled. Rather than eating for fullness (because the foods previously eaten are nutrient robbing and don't provide the fuel for which the body was created), your body will tell you that it's had enough and doesn't need any more. Interesting concept, eh? If you still want foods from the typical American diet, then go ahead and eat them, *but* pay attention to how you feel with and without them. **Connecting the dots** between fuel and how you feel, your mood, your clarity of thought, your energy level, and your ability

to perform your goals is a very important step toward transitioning to a health-building lifestyle.

> ***Note to the DANIEL FAST participants.*** I would encourage you to do this challenge for your first DANIEL FAST rather than "cold turkey" off of all your caffeinated foods and beverages, sugars, processed foods and meat. Removing all your nutrient-robbing foods and adding all the nutrient-dense foods can send you into a cleanse that can be very uncomfortable and extremely hard on your body. Unless you are in a health crisis where death is eminent, I would encourage you to take it more slowly. When your church's fast is over, ask the Lord to empower you to make this a lifestyle rather than a 10-day test. The next time you want to participate in a DANIEL FAST with the church, you'll be ready for the next level. See below.

DANIEL'S 10-Day "Crowd Out" CHALLENGE
This challenge will take a person to a new level of health as the chemically laden, energy-robbing foods are crowded out from the diet. For 10 days, you will be eating at a new level. Fresh fruits, veggies, whole grains, purified waters, legumes, nuts and seeds will captivate your world with their nutritional goodness. You will feel the difference as energy is freed up for clearer thinking and enjoyed activities, happier mood, more energy for healing, and deep cleaning the body of stored toxin or disease. You will also gain a renewed hope that you can live a longer, fuller, happier life. Note that you may experience some withdrawal from processed foods, caffeine or food with additives, but this should be minor compared to going cold-turkey. **DANIEL'S "Add To" CHALLENGE** can provide a great first step towards this lifestyle.

DANIEL'S 10-Day "Super Charge" CHALLENGE
This challenge is for the daring super heroes who want to go beyond their wildest dreams. For 10 days, eat only *raw, living, nutrient packed* foods. You will experience your body's highest level of clarity, spirituality, interpersonal relationships, productivity, joy and hope. Unbelievable!

Empower Your Purpose: The Daniel FEAST! - Lesson Six

DANIEL's "Game On" Scoreboard - Individual

DAY	1	2	3	4	5	6	7	8	9	10	TOTAL POINTS
MEALS (10-pts. per meal; 30 total per day)											
Daily total											
EXERCISE (20 points)											
SLEEP (20 points) 7+ hours											
WATER (10 points)											
BEGIN A NEW HABIT (30 points)											
COMMUNICATION WITH YOUR TEAM (30 points)											
REVIEW HEALTH BUILDING SCRIPTURES & VOCABULARY (50 points)											
PENALTIES (deduct x # of points per penalty):											
BREAKING THE RULES OF THE CHALLENGE (deduct 25)											-
FOCUSING ON FOOD MORE THAN RELATIONSHIPS AND LIFE WORK (deduct 25)											-
FOCUSING ON NUTRIENT ROBBING FOODS INSTEAD OF NUTRIENT RICH FOODS (deduct 25)											-
ALCOHOL (deduct 25)											-
NOT CONNECTING WITH YOUR TEAM (deduct 25)											-
SUB TOTAL FOR THE CHALLENGE											
Bonus Points: If 75% of your team has earned 200 points for 7 or more days then add another 2,000 points to your team's total.											
TOTAL POINTS FOR THE WEEK											

DANIEL's "Game On" Scoreboard - Team

Level 1	Acquire A Taste/Got Juice	TOTAL POINTS	
Level 2	Add To/Not Take Away	TOTAL POINTS	
Level 3	Crowd It Out	TOTAL POINTS	
Level 4	Above & Beyond	TOTAL POINTS	
	TOTAL POINTS FOR THE GAME		

Now that the teams and point systems are set, choose a prize. A relationship-building one (such as an activity) would be ideal, as the reward shouldn't be a financial burden. But if that's not an issue with your group, and you choose to do so, then celebrate big!

Now that you've **connected your dots** by assessing where you are in your health-building journey and you know steps that you can take to successfully build your health, you're GREATLY EMPOWERED to become a victorious member of the transitional generation. Like our time-tested role model, Daniel,  you will courageously dare to test the present lifestyle of the culture. Embracing a bigger picture of long-term results, you will note how your health contributes or distracts from your purpose in life and the purpose of those with whom you do life. By defining your "V" and setting your nutrient packing, healthy lifestyle goals, you can begin your **DANIEL CHALLENGE** with a confidence that you are <u>not</u> missing out on one single thing of *lasting* value. Your focus will be on all the  wonderful, vibrant, beautiful, life-giving foods that you have missed out on prior to *Daniel's* lifestyle and the great relationships that will deepen as you enjoy this journey together! The Daniel Fast will undergo a **paradigm shift**; for truly it is, the Daniel FEAST. No more will you suffer from fun that harms, but will celebrate abundant living with fun that lasts! Congratulations ... and Game On!!!!!

Scriptures to Remember:

"[Not in your own strength] for it is God Who is all the while effectually at work in you [energizing and creating in you the power and desire], both to will and to work for His good pleasure and satisfaction and delight." Philippians 2:13 (AMP)

*"I came that they may have **life**, and have it **abundantly**."*
John 10:10b (NASB, emphasis mine)

Assignment: Pray about how to rearrange your schedule to accommodate joining a DANIEL CHALLENGE. Work your way through all four challenges. Then settle into the one that best fits with your goals.

Start NOW! Drink Reverse Osmosis, distilled, or ionized water (such as Kangen Water®). Avoid spring water or tap water. Drink upon rising in the morning and *in between* meals rather than *with* your meals for best digestion.

Ten times better!

APPENDIX 1
(Introduction)

Three sets of statistics have been provided for you here. As you read through these, think about yourself, your own family system (those for whom you are responsible), and how these stats affect everyone through cost of insurance, time off work, debt from surgeries and other health care costs, as well as safety in the community when people are under stress from financial woes and not feeling well.

1. **These first statistics were compiled in 2003 when I wrote the original guidebook for *DANIEL & Company...Naturally!*** I decided to include them for two reasons: 1) In and of themselves, they are shocking. 2) They give you resources for comparing how nearly decades of amazing advances in medicine are still *not* solving the health crisis.

-Physical Statistics-

Americans spend $98 billion on Health Care and still lead the world in:

- ☒ **HEART DISEASE**
- ☒ **CANCER**
- ☒ **DIABETES**
- ☒ **STROKE**

Although modern health care professionals are now able to keep mankind alive longer than at the turn of the century, the *average American* will live with a **Chronic Degenerative Disease for 20 years** before death. (Dr. Joel Robbins quoted these statistics during course work at the College of Natural Health.)

Ten times better!

Catastrophic Disease in America is an Epidemic!

Every single day in America 8,000 people die from disease. That's 56,000 in one week. *(That's more American deaths than what occurred during the 10 years of the Vietnam War.)*

According to the American Health Ranking, the U.S. spends over two trillion dollars a year (1/6 of our economy, which is more per person than any other nation) on health care. We rank far lower than many developed nations in infant mortality and life expectancy. Japan leads the world with a life expectancy of 75 years, while the U.S. only maintains a life expectancy of 69 years.

Facts:

- This year, one out of every two deaths will be from **heart disease.** (And the first symptom for 1/3 of them will be death!)

- One out of three deaths will be from **cancer.**

- 4,000,000 women are considered **infertile.**

- Two out of seven pregnancies end in **miscarriage.**

- One in ten babies will be born with either **physical or mental handicaps.**

- Over 70% of American women over 17 years of age suffer from either:
    - ☒ **ADD**
    - ☒ **CHRONIC FATIGUE**

Empower Your Purpose: The Daniel FEAST!

- ☒ **DEPRESSION**
- ☒ **PMS**
- ☒ **FIBROMYALGIA**

➢ The number of **OVERWEIGHT KIDS** is doubling every ten years!

➢ Every year in America, two million more people become **DANGEROUSLY OVERWEIGHT** or **OBESE**!

➢ Being **OVERWEIGHT** contributes to over 60 diseases.

➢ If you are 10-20 pounds overweight and do not cleanse on a regular basis, it is not a matter of **IF** you will contract one of these diseases but **WHEN**?

➢ The percentage of overweight people has dramatically increased since **1935** at only **20%** to an astonishing **75%** overweight in the year **2000**:

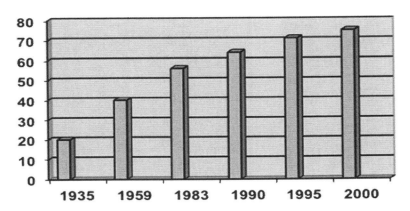

(Statistics obtained from the Center for Disease Control, National Health Museum, National Institute of Health, N.F.S.A., Center for Women's Research.)

2. **The following statistics were obtained prior to the 2009 revision of this book.** As you consider them, notice the numbers from other countries.

Ten times better!

The World Health Organization Statistical Information System (2004) reported that the United States leads the world in deaths from heart disease with 23,761 deaths per year with Germany coming in second with 13,253 deaths per year. Thailand came in 58th with 3 deaths per year. Likewise, the United States leads the world in deaths from diabetes with 50,181 deaths per year. Thailand came in 11th in the world in deaths from diabetes with 4,244 deaths per year and the Cayman Islands only had five deaths per year from diabetes.

According to United Health Foundation and American Health Ranking, the prevalence of obesity rose 127% from 11.6 in 1990 to 26.3% in 2008: "Citizens of the United States are clearly more obese than those of other countries, often more than twice the rate of other countries." "One big reason, our equation for what makes good health has fallen out of calibration. We focus on 'sick care' to make the ill well."

Also according to the American Health Ranking, the United States spends over two trillion dollars a year on health care (1/6th of our economy – more per person than any other nation on earth). We rank far lower than many developed countries in infant mortality and life expectancy. Japan leads the world with a life expectancy of 75 years of age with the United States lower on the list with a life expectancy of 69 years of age.

Oklahoma, my home state, ranks 43rd in the nation for good health. Since 1990 the percentage of obese citizens in Oklahoma rose 148% from 11.6% to 28.8% of the population. Twenty-five point eight percent of Oklahomans smoke. On an average, Oklahomans use 4.1 Poor Physical Health Days and 3.9 Poor Mental Health Days out of 30. Oklahoma was ranked in the bottom three states for least overall improvement in health from 1990 to 2008.

Bottom line (author's note): Spending on health care grew from over 98 billion dollars a year in 2003 to over two trillion dollars a year in 2008 and still didn't fix the illness problem. With the proposed Obama Care, we are projected to spend over three trillion dollars a year. We advocate the cliché here, "Doing the same thing over and over and expecting different results is 'insanity'".

3. **The most up-to-date stats I have included in this revision were obtained from Dr. Linda Heflin, M.D. on "Day 3" of the "Cleanse America" Challenge.** Dr. Heflin was being interviewed by Penni Shelton on *The State of Our Health* (April 11, 2012).

<u>Penni Shelton:</u> "Linda Heflin, M.D. is a family physician, who has been in practice for nearly 20 years. Dr. Heflin has always had a heart for the wellness and prevention aspect of healthcare…"

<u>Dr. Heflin</u> reports to Penni that she is part of a full-service family practice setting. She taught medical students and residents. They are seeing chronic problems at a younger age now. Eight months ago she became very discouraged. Every fourth patient she saw had a chronic disease. She didn't feel that she was helping anyone. She wanted to reverse these persistent problems and educate the families to prevent these diseases for others. She began searching for answers. She saw pictures at *Barefoot Market* and their advertisement for a Raw Food Cooking Class. She didn't know what to think of it. She wondered if that included raw meat? She was intrigued.

Then Dr. Heflin found *Raw Food Rehab* and its founder Penni Shelton of Tulsa, Oklahoma. She began to follow the *Cleanse America* group. She watched the show *Forks Over Knives* that was presented by a PhD and a physician. There she saw the proof she needed to stay on this pathway. They gave sound research gathered over a twelve-year period. They were seeing the reversal of diabetes and heart disease. Dr. Heflin believed there was validity to this. She saw that it was healthy for the planet as well as one's health. All of this together changed the way she currently practices on a day-to-day basis.

Dr. Heflin shares why this is important from a medical standpoint. She states that 40% of Americans are obese. Two out of three Americans are overweight (66%). She states, "We have an epidemic on our hands here." Children are being diagnosed as obese. Obesity leads towards diabetes and is a leading contributor of premature death. Diabetes is the second leading cause of preventable death. Diabetes is second only to cigarette smoking. One in five people in America have hypertension. One in six have heart disease. Eight percent are running around with cancer (25,000,000). Twenty-seven percent have type II diabetes (one in four). One of three people born today will have diabetes in their lifetime. Half of America is on prescription drugs. How many of them are on more than one? People age 45 and over currently have a 60% chance (if the diet isn't changed) to have two to three chronic diseases by age 45. In 2006 at the International Congress on Obesity, they completed a study that revealed that, for the first time in the history of the planet, there are more people who are obese (over 1 billion) than there are who are hungry in the world (estimated 600 to 700,000,000).

I received these two pictures in an email. The message that came with it was something to the effect that the Statue of David was on loan to the United States. After some time in the U.S., it was returned in the following condition.

 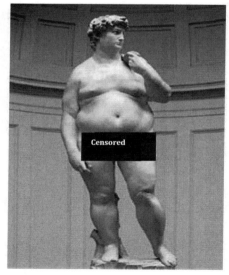

APPENDIX 2
(Lesson One)

If you are the more detailed, organized and "Type A" person, then the following are some wonderful resources for your charting enjoyment. Don't let the amount of chart options overwhelm you. Frame them as the super abundant provision of the Creator to help you be victorious. Use what interests you, and leave the rest. Different strokes for different folks!

CONNECTING YOUR DOTS
Identify Your Symptoms

Clearly spell out the **symptoms** you're experiencing. For example, under **Physical** you might write, *I am 25 pounds overweight and have a family history of diabetes* or *I consume energy drinks and lots of caffeine just to function throughout the day* or *I always seem to be tired and in need of a nap.* Under **Emotional** or **Spiritual** you might write, *I seem to struggle with insecurity and a lack of peace* or *I'm mad at God about my health* or *Why doesn't God do something?*

Physical	Emotional	Spiritual

Ten times better!

CONNECTING YOUR DOTS
Recognize the Consequences

What happens if you don't listen to your body and heed the warnings from your symptoms? For example, under **Physical** you may write, *My spouse has indicated that he will always love me no matter what, but he is struggling with being attracted to me with the extra weight I've put on; I don't want to be unappealing to the one I love* or *Research shows that being overweight contributes to over 60 known diseases* or *My doctor has warned me that I am at risk for heart disease or a heart attack, and I certainly don't want to go on expensive medications for the rest of my life or undergo surgery.* Under **"Emotional"** or **"Spiritual"** you may write, *I know this is counterproductive to healthy relationships - human and spiritual - and I may end up rejecting God and be rejected by my family and friends, thus very alone in the world.*

Physical	Emotional	Spiritual

Transition to "Dots" that lead to
Physical and Relational HEALTH

What do you want to achieve? This should be the opposite of the symptom(s) you listed. For example, under **Physical** you may write, *Although I have put on an extra 25 pounds I'm not going to focus on losing weight. I'm going to focus on applying the DANIEL LIFESTYLE truths and see what weight my body tells me is good for me. I'm excited to see the weight drop off, as I know a healthy body is the right size. I want the energy back that I'm giving away by carrying around this extra weight, and I want to become more attractive to my spouse.* Under **Emotional** you may write, *Like our role model, DANIEL, I will watch for opportunities to learn more about who I am, where I am to make my contribution, and additional relational skills so I can most effectively stay connected with others.* Under **"Spiritual"** you may write, *I will evaluate my relationship with my Creator and consider ways to grow in my understanding of spiritual truths for I realize they translate into physical and relational beauty.*

Physical	Emotional	Spiritual

APPENDIX 3
(Lesson One and Lesson Five)

How Food & Family Have Changed Over Time

Between 1900 & 1980:

- Whole grain dropped 50%
- <u>Fresh</u> fruit & vegetables dropped from 40% to 20%
- Citrus fruit dropped 33%
- Sugar increased 50%
- <u>Processed</u> fruit & vegetables ↑ 400%

In the 1940's:

- 10% of the food we ate was processed

Between 1940 & 1980:

- Food coloring consumption ↑ 90%

Between 1960 & 1980:

- Soft drink consumption ↑ 300%

In the 1990's:

- 90% of the food we ate was processed

In the 2000's:

- We eat 10 pounds of toxic additives per person per year
- 91 cents out of every dollar is spent on processed foods

What was happening during this time?

- World War I
- World War II
- Korea
- Vietnam, etc.
- The "Great Generation" was fighting for life

Where were the women during the wars?

Initially, the women were in the traditional role in the home caring for the nurturing and nutrition of the children. In his book, *The Best War Ever*, Michael C. C. Adams (professor of history, and chair of history and geography at Northern Kentucky University) writes that the traditional role of women was changing:

*There was "...a government business campaign to get married women to do paid work, reversing the conventional wisdom that said a wife should be a full-time homemaker. By 1942, the white male unemployment pool had dried up, and new worker groups were needed. **Married white women** were the most obvious labor source, and so propaganda badgered and enticed them into the labor market. **'Mrs. Stay-at-Home'** was the target of one ad saying that women were **not doing their share**."*

*A 1943 editorial in the <u>Baltimore News Post</u> told unemployed wives: **"Sister you'd better reform."***

*<u>The War Manpower Commission</u> asserted that, "...women have been allowed to fall into **habits of extraordinary leisure**" and were "**getting by just being** a 'good wife and mother'."*

Women were also told that they had "...over-parented their children" and that "'mom-ism' (the spoiling of male adolescents) was responsible for the high failure rate of army inductees to reach basic physical and mental standards of toughness."

The upshot was an influx of married women into the job market. In 1944, for the first time, married female workers outnumbered single female workers, representing 72 percent of the increase in employed women since 1940. By then, 19 million women had paid jobs. We should not exaggerate the extent of real change that this represented...

Not everyone supported women being war workers. Conservative journals such as <u>American Home</u> and the <u>Catholic Commonwealth</u> urged women to stay home... Many women felt great guilt about shirking their family responsibilities and tried to do two jobs, one in and one out of the home. They got some help from daycare centers for infants, but these were often expensive and inconvenient, and they carried a stigma of parental neglect, so most women relied on family help with children and worked hard to accommodate both family and employer.

One woman, who worked nights, got home at 7:30 a.m. After a short sleep, she got up to shop, clean, wash clothes, and cook for her husband and daughter. Another rose at 5:45 a.m. to cook the family breakfast before punching in at work at 7:00 a.m. Some nights, if she didn't manage to get dinner on the table by six o'clock, her husband "was mad". Food stores were asked to stay open one night a week to enable women workers to shop. By early 1944, the strain on working women had led to high absenteeism.

When it became clear, late in 1944, that the war was being won and that women were no longer needed in the work force, the media began encouraging women to return home, partly **because of a growing fear that children were being neglected**. The worry was no longer about "mom-ism" but about the emotional and behavior problems of unsupervised adolescents.

*Both the Depression and the war appeared to lessen parental authority...**Fathers and elder brothers were often away at war, so important role models were lost**. If the **mother worked too**, the **stage seemed set** for wildness among **unsupervised** children. Adults worried about adolescent hostility and rebellion, which was expressed in growing numbers of street gangs.*

Cutting school increased; in Detroit, truancy jumped 24 percent between 1938 and 1943. More girls got pregnant. And the venereal disease rate rose: between 1941 and 1944, New York City's venereal disease rate among girls aged fifteen to eighteen years old increased 204 percent ... they threw drinking parties and stayed up all night smoking cigarettes and reefers. ... Some youths joined gangs and there was a rash of vandalism, such as slashing seats on public transport and stealing cars to joyride ... Of most concern to the white middle class, the rise in crime rate for white youth outpaced that for black youth by 250 percent.

*What was happening? Studies suggested that business prosperity and juvenile delinquency moved in the same direction ... unrestricted freedom and power, which produced immature or wild behavior ... being a consumer did not give **life a purpose**: American youth were **bored and at loose ends**, a recipe for problems.*

*The ultimate difficulty was that, prosperous and unfettered as they might be, juveniles were outside the great events taking place. They were peripheral to the war effort and often **felt slighted**. Adolescents were attracted to personal freedom and yet **yearned to be useful in the larger world** ... The anger created by feeling small and foolish was one cause of delinquency, **as frustrated teens provoked adults to get their attention.***

Just as disturbing for America's stability was a perceived decline in family values. "Are we facing a moral breakdown?" was by 1945 a favorite radio talk show topic. Delinquency continued to rise, as did divorce, with half a million breakups in 1945. Many of these failed relationships came out of unique wartime circumstances: young women had felt moral pressure to marry a GI and send him overseas happy.

Often such whirlwind romances, fuelled by the adrenaline flow of war, could not survive sustained separation or the reality of daily contact in the flatter atmosphere of peace. Where couples were clearly incompatible, these war marriages were best ended. But critics also saw in the statistics **a decline in American values and identified as the major culprit women working outside the home during the war.**

A 1945 State Farm Insurance ad showed a hysterical girl being carted away to a foster home because her mother was out working. Women were urged to leave their jobs, which would then be available for returning veterans, and to **focus on restoring a healthy home life.**

The gratitude toward women, for their contribution to the war effort, stopped short of according them full legal equality. In 1945 the Equal Rights Amendment failed in the U.S. Senate. As the war ended, a disproportionate number of women workers were laid off. Many accepted this cheerfully, but others felt betrayed by the turnaround. A fired woman worker at the Tacoma Navy Yard said, "Many women in here are plenty unhappy though. The taste of independence has spoiled 'em".

Focus on the Family, August 2001: If you had to indicate the one factor that has done more damage to families than any other, what would it be?

> **Dr. Dobson**: It would be the almost universal condition of **fatigue** and **time pressure,** which leaves every member of the family exhausted and harried. Many of them have nothing left to invest in their marriages or in the nurturing of children. Some of these young women grew up in busy, dysfunctional,

career-oriented households, and they **want something better for their kids.** *And yet* **financial pressures and the expectations of others** *keep them on a treadmill that renders them unable to cope. I have never said publicly what I will share now - and I will be criticized for saying so in this context - but I believe the two-career family during the child rearing years* **creates a level of stress that is tearing people apart. And it often deprives children of something that they will search for, for the rest of their lives.**

If a scale-back from this lifestyle, which I call 'routine panic', ever grows into a **movement, it will portend wonderfully for the family. It should result in fewer divorces, more domestic harmony, children will regain the status they deserve, and their welfare will be enhanced on a thousand fronts.**

We haven't begun to approach these goals yet, but I pray that a significant segment of the population will awaken someday from the nightmare of over commitment and say, "The way we live is crazy. There has to be a better way than this to raise our kids. We will make the financial sacrifices necessary to slow the pace of living."

His Needs Her Needs - Willard F. Harley, Jr.

Any husband can make himself irresistible to his wife by learning to meet her five most important emotional needs:

1. *Affection*
2. *Conversation*
3. *Honesty and openness*
4. *Financial support*
5. *Family commitment*

Ten times better!

> *Likewise, a wife makes herself irresistible to her husband by learning to meet his five most important emotional needs:*
>
> 1. *Sexual fulfillment*
> 2. *Recreational companionship*
> 3. *Physical attractiveness*
> 4. *Domestic support**
> 5. *Admiration*

* She creates a home that offers him a refuge from the stresses of life. She manages the household responsibilities in a way that encourages him to spend time at home enjoying his family.

APPENDIX 4
(Lesson One)

Family System Evaluation

Where does your family system fit into the national statistics?

Relational

___# of divorces/separations in your family (including extended family)

What affect does it have on the family?

_____
_____
_____
_____

Physical

___# of family members dying of chronic degenerative disease.

How long do you recall each of them living with the disease before death?

_____
_____
_____
_____

APPENDIX 5
(Lesson Two)

Peter's Vision:
The Sheet of Unclean Animals

This passage in Acts 10 was included because many people mistakenly believe it is a license to eat anything they may want. However, upon more careful examination, one can see that this passage is not about food as Peter originally thought, but rather it is guiding Peter to *accept men* of all race, not just Jewish ones.

Acts 10 (MSG) *About noon ... Peter went up on the roof to pray. He became hungry and wanted something to eat, and while the meal was being prepared, he fell into a trance. He saw heaven opened and something like a large sheet being let down to earth by its four corners. It contained all kinds of four-footed animals as well as reptiles of the earth, and birds of the air. Then a voice told him,* "Get up, Peter. Kill and eat."

"Surely not, Lord!" Peter replied, **"I have never eaten anything impure or unclean."**

The voice spoke to him a second time, **"Do not call anything impure that God has made clean."**

This happened three times, and immediately the sheet was taken back to heaven.

While **Peter was still thinking about the vision,** *the Spirit said to him, "Simon, three* **men** *are looking for you. So get up and go downstairs.* **Do not hesitate to go with them, for I have sent them.**"

The men replied, "We have come from Cornelius the centurion. He is a righteous and God-fearing man, who is respected by all the Jewish people. A holy angel told him to have you come to his house so that he could hear what you have to say."

Peter responded to them in verse 27. ... *But God has shown me that I should not call any **man** impure or unclean.*

Peter emphasizes the meaning of the message again in verse 34. *Then Peter began to speak: "I now realize how true it is that God does not show favoritism, but **accepts men from every nation** who fear him and do what is right."*

APPENDIX 6
(Lesson Three)

DANIEL CHALLENGE REPLACEMENT PLAN
Replacing Nutrient Robbing with Nutrient Rich

Consider what your typical weekly menu looks like. Next, choose a timeframe in which you think you can realistically transition toward a nutrient rich food plan. Using the lists below, you will find replacements for the nutrient robbing foods you have been consuming. **Even if it means you only replace one ingredient at each meal, you are still moving in the right direction toward healthy living.** We have created Journal Pages for your convenience in working with these lists.

	Nutrient Robbing	Nutrient Rich
Beverages	Alcohol, coffee, tea, cocoa, carbonated beverages and soft drinks (including sports drinks), all commercial juices containing preservatives, refined salt, sweeteners.	Freshly extracted vegetable juices, BarleyMax, CarrotJuiceMax, BeetMax, distilled water, caffeine-free herb teas, cereal-based coffee beverages, bottled organic juices.
Dairy to Dairy Alternatives	All animal-based milk, cheese, eggs, ice cream, whipped toppings, non-dairy creamers. You may find it helpful to add an extra step to your transition by going from products made from cow to products made from goat, then on to non-dairy products.	Fresh milk derived from oats, rice, coconut, nuts such as almond and hazelnut. Also "fruit creams" made from strawberry, banana, blueberry. Non-dairy cheese and milk, almond milk, nut butters.
Fruits	Canned and sweetened fruits, as well as non-organic dried fruits.	All fresh, as well as organic "unsulphered" dried fruit, stewed/frozen unsweetened fruits.

Grains	Refined, bleached-flour products, cold breakfast cereals, white rice.	Soaked oats, millet, raw muesli, dehydrated granola or crackers, raw ground flaxseed. Whole grain cereals, breads, muffins, pasta, brown rice, spelt, amaranth, millet, etc.
Meats to Beans	Beef, pork, fish, chicken, turkey, hamburgers, hot dogs, bacon, sausage, etc.	Green beans, peas, sprouted garbanzo beans, sprouted lentils, sprouted mung, lima, adzuki, black, kidney, navy, pinto, red, white, and other dried beans.
Nuts/Seeds	All roasted and/or salted seeds, nuts.	Raw almonds, sunflower seeds, macadamia nuts, walnuts, raw almond butter, tahini.
Oil to Oils & Fats	All lard, margarine, shortenings; anything containing hydrogenated oils.	Extra virgin olive oil, grapeseed oil for cooking, Udo's Choice Perfected Oil Blend, flaxseed oil, avocados, mayonnaise made from cold-pressed oils.
Seasonings	Refined table salt, black pepper, any seasonings containing them.	All fresh, dried and dehydrated herbs, garlic, sweet onions, parsley, salt-free seasonings, light gray unrefined sea salt, cayenne pepper.
Soups	All canned or packaged soups, creamed soups that contain dairy products.	Raw soups, soups made from scratch – without fat, dairy, table salt.
Sweets	All refined white or brown sugar, sugar syrups, chocolate, candy, gum, cookies, donuts, cakes, pies, other products containing refined sugars or artificial sweeteners.	Fruit smoothies, raw fruit pies with date/nut crusts, date/nut squares. Raw, unfiltered honey, rice syrup, unsulphered molasses, stevia, carob, pure maple syrup, date sugar.
Vegetables	All canned vegetables with added preservatives or vegetables fried in oil.	All raw vegetables, steamed/wok-cooked fresh or frozen vegetables, baked white or sweet potatoes, squash, etc.

Ten times better!

DANIEL CHALLENGE REPLACEMENT JOURNAL

DAY ONE: _____

BREAKFAST	LUNCH	DINNER
Replace:	Replace:	Replace:
With:	With:	With:

DAY TWO: _____

BREAKFAST	LUNCH	DINNER
Replace:	Replace:	Replace:
With:	With:	With:

DAY THREE: _____

BREAKFAST	LUNCH	DINNER
Replace:	Replace:	Replace:
With:	With:	With:

DAY FOUR: _____

BREAKFAST	LUNCH	DINNER
Replace:	Replace:	Replace:
With:	With:	With:

DAY FIVE: _____

BREAKFAST	**LUNCH**	**DINNER**
Replace:	Replace:	Replace:
With:	With:	With:

DAY SIX: _____

BREAKFAST	**LUNCH**	**DINNER**
Replace:	Replace:	Replace:
With:	With:	With:

DAY SEVEN: _____

BREAKFAST	**LUNCH**	**DINNER**
Replace:	Replace:	Replace:
With:	With:	With:

DAY EIGHT: _____

BREAKFAST	**LUNCH**	**DINNER**
Replace:	Replace:	Replace:
With:	With:	With:

Ten times better!

DAY NINE: _____		
BREAKFAST	**LUNCH**	**DINNER**
Replace:	Replace:	Replace:
With:	With:	With:

DAY TEN: _____		
BREAKFAST	**LUNCH**	**DINNER**
Replace:	Replace:	Replace:
With:	With:	With:

APPENDIX 7
(Lessons Three and Six)

Budget Worksheet*

INCOME SOURCES

    Salary   _____
    Interest   _____
    Dividends   _____
    Rents   _____
    Notes   _____
    Income Tax Refund   _____
    Other   _____

    TOTAL   _____

OUTGO

    Tithe   _____
    Federal Income Tax   _____
    State Income Tax   _____
    Federal Social Security Tax   _____

    Housing Expense……………...36%**
    Rent   _____
     Residence Tax   _____
     Residence Insurance   _____

    Food……………………...12%   _____
    Auto……………...…………..12%   _____
    Outstanding debt……………..05%   _____

Ten times better!

```
Insurance (Life, Health, Auto)..05%    _____
Clothes Allowance....................05%    _____
Medical/ Dental...................04%    _____
Savings...........................05%    _____
Investing.........................05%    _____
Miscellaneous.....................05%    _____
School/Child Care................06%    _____
```

*These figures are ones I have used with Crown Financial Services back when it was under Larry Burkett's name. See www.crownfinancial.org for more information. Dave Ramsey's Financial Peace University is another great resource. See them at www.daveramsey.com/fpu

**These are percentages of the net spend-able after tithe and taxes.

APPENDIX 8
(Lesson Three)

CRAVINGS

Cravings don't always affect your mood, but they definitely can - before *and* after you satisfy them or if you *don't* satisfy them. Thus, they can affect your relationships -- significantly. Therefore, it is very important to understand them and know how best to work with them.

When you first begin following the dietary recommendations you usually find that, after a day or two (or sometimes longer), you are craving everything that should not be eaten. ***Do not be discouraged by this;*** it is a *normal* occurrence and is due to a physiological change in the body's chemistry.

It is recommended that during this time you **don't** become militant against the craving, trying to resist and not submit to it. Instead, take a positive approach. Ask yourself:

- **Have I had any fresh juice today?**
- **Have I had a salad today?**
- **Have I had any fruit today?**
- **Have I had a green drink today?**
- **Have I had any nuts or seeds today?**
- **Have I connected with God, family or friends today?**
- **Am I fulfilling my purpose today?**

Ten times better!

If you have satisfied your nutrition and nurture needs and still want what you are craving, then go ahead and eat whatever the craving dictates.

Cravings can be great teachers. They can help you discover why you like certain health-harming foods and cause you to seek healthy replacements that crowd them out. **Ask yourself what it is about the craving that you like so much. Then seek answers to what you could eat or do that would meet that need in a health building way. Watch your body's response to what you ate and note how it affected you. Connect those dots. This is very important. The GREAT LIE is that those cravings are GOOD. We've just GOT to get smart here. We must mature. We must understand what they are doing to us and redefine "good" to what is good in the *long run*. Get back on the health-building track tomorrow.** Do not feel guilty when you eat the "no-no's." Keep in mind that you are not on a diet; therefore, **you cannot 'fail your diet'**. Rather, **you are developing a new *lifestyle*,** and growing in your understanding and maturity. We cannot change lifelong habits

overnight. Simply improve your diet a little each month. Don't fight your cravings; work with them. Even plan for them.

In a few weeks you will learn about the "Miracle in Wisconsin", and how an adjusted diet drastically improved the health, attention, mood and education of students in an alternative school. Once a month these students have a junk food day to remind them of why they transitioned to healthy diets. On those days, they document how the junk foods affect their ability to think, produce good work, and their mood. You may find the same holds true for you!

"There is therefore **no condemnation** to those who are in Christ Jesus." (Romans 8:1 KJV) Could this mean, "Those who are in the learning process with Christ Jesus?"

The days of "craving" the health-robbing foods will become fewer and further between as time goes on. Also, you will notice as time passes that your craving will slowly subside because these foods will **not taste as good as you remember them to be**, and in time you will become sick when you eat them.

As the body chemistry becomes healthier, it rejects the bad food and enjoys health-producing foods. Then you will notice your cravings **change** to the good foods. In one year, you will look back and be *amazed* at how far you have progressed, and of course will reap the health benefits that go with the improved diet.

PERSONAL NOTE: I have never told my husband that he could not have a particular food. #1) That's not my place to do so. His diet is his responsibility. #2) Our goal is to have everything we want -- by helping our "wanter" mature. Our "wanter" will show its maturity when it makes smart decisions. Smart decisions are ones that will produce lasting benefits to us, and those our lives affect.

APPENDIX 9
(Lesson Three)

Guide to Soaking Nuts and Seeds

If a recipe calls for soaked nuts or seeds, measure them after soaking. Remember, we are soaking, pouring off the soaking water, and then dehydrating them before using because they have an enzyme inhibitor in them that makes them harder to digest. Therefore, preparing them this way increases the energy ratio between the amounts of energy received from the food versus the amount of energy it costs to digest and assimilate it.

Nut or Seed	Dry Amount	Soaking Time	Yield Soaked
Almond	1 cup	8-12 hours	1 ½ cups
Walnut	1 cup	4-6 hours	1 ¼ cups
Pecan	1 cup	4-6 hours	1 ¼ cups
Sunflower seeds	1 cup	6-8 hours	1 1/3 cups
Sesame seeds	1 cup	4-6 hours	1 ¼ cups
Cashews	1 cup	2 hours	1 cup

APPENDIX 10
(Lesson Four)

Additional Tips for Finicky or Reluctant Eaters

I have worked with many different groups of people - young/old, rich/poor, and the athletic/more technical types. The following are some techniques I have used to help them try real foods.

Model it first and don't let them try it. Teach them the **benefits**. Teach them the **harm** if they don't. Teach them **manners** when someone is trying to help them. It is highly offensive to say, "Yuck! Eeeeew," turn your head or walk away. They should treat those offering to help them with respect and appreciation.

So, how did that play out when I was working with three 6A public school basketball teams? (These were primarily of the socioeconomic system titled **Free and Reduced Lunch**.) Every one of them tried the carrot, lemon, apple juice and whole grain breads I brought in to them.

They even came back for thirds until it was ALL gone, AND sneaked in some of the football players to try it, too!

When we were introducing the juicing to my sons, some of them played JV and Varsity basketball. Between games I would bring them fresh juice. I put it in a covered mug so the other team members wouldn't see the color and become tempted to tease. It became known as **"Go Juice"** and **"Gwartney Juice"** (my sons' last name).

Now that we have grandchildren, my sons and daughters-in-law have allowed the wee ones to help make it. Somehow, taking ownership of the juice makes it something they want. Again, use a covered cup and bright colored straw and you've got a treasured gourmet drink. The children have given it different names such as **"Afton Juice"** (like "Gwartney Juice", only using her first name) and **"Orange Juice"**, the name given to our signature drink of carrot, lemon, and apple (because of the color, not the contents). Inviting extended family and friends over for an evening of making and tasting new juices can prove enjoyable, entertaining and beneficial. This works well with babies, school age, college, and young adults – it doesn't matter the age. We can turn food prep into a fun, learning, and social activity.

With our wee ones, we also play **Happy Drink**. We use little bitty "shot" glasses. (Some people may feel uncomfortable with this, as shot glasses are typically used with alcohol, however in the natural health arena a "shot" of wheat grass is common and not considered "leading people astray." We claim all the tools we can to help children accept "Green Drinks", i.e. barley drinks.) Emphasize that only "big kids" get to play this game. We let them help make the drink by holding on to the personal hand mixer, with adult help, while watching for the "tornado" that forms as the agave and green drink make their respective brown and green tornados. Then we pour the drink into little glasses and everyone clicks glasses and says, "Cheers, Happy Drink!" and again, "Cheers, Happy Drink!" They think it's such fun that they will continue to do it over and over until it is all gone -- and then they ask for more!

We play a similar game at the dinner table when there is a finicky wee one who may not like a certain taste or texture. It's called **The Big Boy/Girl Game**. One person starts the game by saying something to the affect, "I'm so glad we get to eat _____ (name the item) because it _____ (name what it does for them.)" Then the person goes on to say something like "I didn't like it at first, but as I've gotten more grown up and my tastes have changed, I really love it now. It makes me feel so good!" Then another person at the table will say something similar. After everyone who wants to play participates, the finicky one is invited to either wait until the next time the food is served when they are "bigger," or they are invited to try it on the spot (whichever seems appropriate). If the wee one starts to make a yucky sound or face, he/she is reminded of their manners and encouraged that as he/she grows up he/she will learn to like it since it's so good for "our" bodies. It does little good to create a negative memory while learning to eat something new.

"For the wrath of man worketh not the righteousness of God"
James 1:20 (KJV)

Another fun game that has proven affective is the **Nutrient Packing Wheel.** You can use the wheel for juicing, smoothies, sandwiches, pastas, stir fries, pizzas, etc. This is how it works: someone chooses the meal item, and then each person chooses what he or she would like to add to the main item. Let's use "pizza" for this illustration. Each person can customize a section of the pizza to their preferences and then create a section as a "family or friendship piece". On this piece they put ingredients that everyone likes. When deepening the intimacy in relationships, one can learn to like the things that delight those one loves. I personally have learned to love herbs, teas, vegetables, textures, temperatures, etc. just for social and relational reasons. There are more reasons for eating than just to please one's own palate.

With older, more sophisticated types of people, education and presentation are the keys. Talk about the Blue Zone and the fact that people are living disease free and productive until they are one hundred years old and dying peacefully. Educate them as to what the food item is that you wish them to try, to what it is similar in taste, and how it will benefit them. Serve it on a beautiful dish with garnish for a classy, respectful presentation. Encourage them that tastes change as the body chemistry changes and suggest that they may like to try it again at a later date if they don't care for it. However, more often than not, they will be amazed at the explosion of taste and how "do-able and fun" it is to add these foods to their diet.

Challenge your mature loved one's thinking by helping them connect the dots between fuel and performance, as well as, missed work or low productivity and irritability. Also, expand their thinking to the big picture of the high cost of health care and what legacy they would like to leave in their senior years.

APPENDIX 11
(Lesson Four)

From "Need to Know PBS"
The Dirty Dozen and *Clean 15 of Produce*

These are the produce with the most and least herbicide/pesticide contamination. If the cost of buying all organic isn't within your budget, fear not. (Of course, buying organic is always a good choice for the health of farms and farm workers, regardless of the residue left on the end product.) *The Dirty Dozen* and *Clean 15 of Produce* can guide you until you can purchase all organic. Not mentioned in the list below are the dehydrated foods such as raisins. Of course, they would be best purchased as organics since the drying process would concentrate the chemicals on the dried fruits. Otherwise, see the article and lists below.

Jackie Pou
May 13, 2010

A new report issued by the President's Cancer Panel recommends eating produce without pesticides to reduce your risk of getting cancer and other diseases. And according to the Environmental Working Group (an organization of scientists, researchers and policymakers), certain types of organic produce can reduce the amount of toxins you consume on a daily basis by as much as 80 percent.

The group put together two lists, *The Dirty Dozen* and *The Clean 15*, to help consumers know when they should buy organic and when it is unnecessary. These lists were compiled using data from the United States Department of Agriculture on the amount of pesticide residue found in non-organic fruits and vegetables after they had been washed.

The fruits and vegetables on *The Dirty Dozen* list, when conventionally grown, tested positive for at least 47 different chemicals, with some testing positive for as many as 67. For produce on the "dirty" list, you should definitely go organic — unless you relish the idea of consuming a chemical cocktail. *The Dirty Dozen* list includes:

1. celery
2. peaches
3. strawberries
4. apples
5. domestic blueberries
6. nectarines
7. sweet bell peppers
8. spinach, kale and collard greens
9. cherries
10. potatoes
11. imported grapes
12. lettuce

All the produce on *The Clean 15* bore little to no traces of pesticides, and is safe to consume in non-organic form. This list includes:

1. onions
2. avocados
3. sweet corn
4. pineapples
5. mango
6. sweet peas
7. asparagus
8. kiwi fruit
9. cabbage
10. eggplant

11. cantaloupe
12. watermelon
13. grapefruit
14. sweet potatoes
15. sweet onions

Why are some types of produce more prone to sucking up pesticides than others? Richard Wiles, senior vice president of policy for the Environmental Working Group says, "If you eat something like a pineapple or sweet corn, they have a protection defense because of the outer layer of skin. Not the same for strawberries and berries."

The President's Cancer Panel recommends washing conventionally grown produce to remove residues. Wiles adds, "You should do what you can do, but the idea you are going to wash pesticides off is a fantasy. But you should still wash it because you will reduce pesticide exposure."

Remember, the lists of dirty *and* clean produce were compiled *after* the USDA washed the produce using high-power pressure water systems that many of us could only dream of having in our kitchens.

The full list contains 49 types of produce, rated on a scale of least to most pesticide residue. You can check out the full list from on the Environmental Working Group's website at www.foodnews.org or read more at http://www.thedailygreen.com/healthy-eating/eat-safe/dirty-dozen-foods#ixzz1nmZaCuVL

APPENDIX 12
(Lesson Five)

Monday, October 14, 2003
A MIRACLE IN WISCONSIN

October 14. In Appleton, Wisconsin, a revolution has occurred. It has taken place in the Central Alternative High School. The kids now behave. The hallways aren't frantic. Even the teachers are happy.

The school used to be out of control - kids packed weapons, discipline problems swamped the principal's office - but since 1997, a private group called *Natural Ovens* (http://www.naturalovens.con/new/Valparaiso.htm) began installing a healthy lunch program. (1.800.558.3535)

Fast-food burgers, fries, and burritos gave way to fresh salads, meats "prepared with old-fashioned recipes," and whole grain bread. Fresh fruits were added to the menu. Good drinking water arrived. Vending machines were removed.

As reported in a newsletter called *Pure Facts*, "Grades are up, truancy is no longer a problem, arguments are rare, and teachers are able to spend their time teaching."

Principal Ann Coenen, who files annual reports with the state of Wisconsin, has turned in some staggering figures since 1997. Dropouts? Students expelled? Students discovered to be using drugs? Carrying weapons? Committing suicide? Every category has come up ZERO. Every year.

Mary Bruyette, a teacher, states, "I don't have to deal with daily discipline issues—I don't have disruptions in class or the difficulties with student behavior I experienced before we started the food program."

One student asserted, "Now that I can concentrate I think it's easier to get along with people ..."

What a concept—eating healthier food increases concentration. Principal Coenen sums it up: "I can't buy the argument that it's too costly for schools to provide good nutrition for their students. I've found that one cost will reduce another. I don't have the vandalism. I don't have the litter. I don't have the need for high security."

At a nearby middle school, the new food program is catching on. A teacher there, Dennis Abram, reports, "I've taught there almost 30 years. I see the kids this year as calmer, easier to talk to. They just seem more rational. I had thought about retiring this year and basically I've decided to teach another year—I'm having too much fun!"

Pure Facts, the newsletter that ran this story, is published by a non-profit organization called *The Feingold Association*, which has existed since 1976. Part of its mission is to "generate public awareness of the potential role of foods and synthetic additives in behavior, learning and health problems. The (Feingold) program is based on a diet eliminating synthetic colors, synthetic flavors, and the preservatives BHA, BHT, and TBHQ."

Thirty years ago there was a Dr. Feingold. His breakthrough work proved the connection between these negative factors in food and the lives of children. Hailed as a revolutionary advance, Feingold's findings were soon trashed by the medical cartel, since those findings threatened the drugs-for-everything, disease-model concept of modern healthcare. But Feingold's followers have kept his work alive.

If what happened in Appleton, Wisconsin, takes hold in many other communities across America, perhaps the ravenous corporations who invade school space with their vending machines and junk food will be tossed out on their behinds. It could happen. And perhaps ADHD will become a dinosaur - a non-disease that was once attributed to errant brain chemistry. And perhaps Ritalin will be seen as just another toxic chemical that was added to the bodies of kids in a crazed attempt to put a lid on behavior that, in part, was the result of a subversion of the food supply. For those readers who ask me about solutions to the problems we face, here is a real solution. Help these groups. Get involved. Step into the fray. Stand up and be counted. The drug companies aren't going to do it. They're busy estimating the size of their potential markets. They're building their chemical pipelines into the minds and bodies of the young.

Every great revolution starts with a foothold. Sounds like *Natural Ovens* and *The Feingold Association* have made strong cuts into the big rock of ignorance and greed. Go for it.

****

The Quantum Agriculture Project
2555 Mark West Station Road
Windsor, CA 95492
707.836.0699
shanjam@igc.org

APPENDIX 13
(Lesson Five)

PRAYER FOR SPIRITUAL BIRTH

If you can say this:

It's my understanding that You created everything, including mankind. You created us for fellowship with You and to rule over the Garden of Eden and all that was in it. You long for the joy of *genuine* love from Your creation, thus provided an opportunity for mankind to *choose* whether to trust Your loving design or reject it.

Because mankind chose to reject Your design for us and eat fruit that we were not created to eat (causing a spiritual death to take place and a physical death to begin), You were forced to end fellowship with us in the garden. This protected us from dying in that state should we also choose to eat of the Tree of Life which was also in the Garden of Eden.

But, the wonderful news is, You loved mankind so much that you immediately began the process to rescue us from that dead and dying state and provide opportunity to be "born again" into a spiritual relationship with You. This would reverse spiritual death, and make possible for us to enjoy eternal and abundant life once again.

You did this through the death, burial and resurrection of Your perfect Son, Jesus Christ who paid the legal price for our redemption with his life's blood. Understanding, believing, and acknowledging this before You and others begins this new spiritual life of learning Your ways of abundant life.

Then I invite you to pray the following:

My Creator, My God, My Savior,

I accept the loving gift of redemption by Jesus Christ and receive spiritual life into my body by the indwelling of the Holy Spirit right now. I will follow Your direction to acknowledge You before men in baptism and begin my spiritual maturation process through this life. I love you and thank you for this wonderful opportunity.

> In the Name of the Father, Son, and Holy Spirit,
> Amen.

PRAYER FOR GOD'S HELP AS YOUR CREATOR

Dear Almighty God in Heaven, Maker of the Universe,

I understand that there are many ways to know you; as *Father, Savior, Comforter, Provider, Healer, Deliverer* and many others. Today, I want You to know that I'd like to understand You more fully as my *Creator*. Please teach me how to relate to You this way. I want my life to be all that You designed for it to be. For I do believe that the plans You have for me are good. They are meant to prosper me, to give me a future and hope. Through them I'll experience "fullness of joy" and "pleasures that last." I trust you to finish the work you began in me.

> In Jesus' Name,
> Amen.

APPENDIX 14

Scriptures for Reference and Memorization

Why use Scriptures?

"All Scripture is God-breathed and is valuable for teaching the truth, convicting of sin, correcting faults and training in right living; thus anyone who belongs to God may be fully equipped for every good work." 2 Timothy 3:16 (The Complete Jewish Bible)

*"This book of the law shall not depart out of thy mouth; but thou shalt **meditate** therein day and night, that thou mayest observe to do according to all that is written therein: for then thou shalt make thy way **prosperous**, and then thou shalt have **good success**."* Joshua 1:8 (KJV)

*"Therefore, I urge you, brothers, in view of God's mercy, to offer your bodies as living sacrifices, holy and pleasing to God – this is your spiritual (KJV "reasonable") act of worship. Do not conform any longer to the pattern of this world, **but be transformed by the renewing of your mind**. Then you will be able to test and approve what God's will is – His good, pleasing and perfect will."* Romans 12:1, 2 (NIV)

"Love the Lord your God with all your heart and with all your soul and with all your strength. These commandments that I give you today are to be upon your hearts. Impress them on your children. Talk about them when you sit at home and when you walk along the road, when you lie down and when you get up. Tie them as symbols on your hands and bind them on your foreheads. Write them on the doorframes of your houses and on your gates." Deuteronomy 6:5-9 (NIV)

LESSON 1

"In the beginning God created ..." Genesis 1:1 (NIV)

"So God created man in his own image ..." Genesis 1:27 (NIV)

"For I know the plans I have for you," declares the Lord, "plans to prosper you and not to harm you, plans to give you hope and a future." Jeremiah 29:11 (NIV)

"Thou wilt show me the path of life: in Thy presence is fullness of joy; at Thy right hand there are pleasures for evermore." Psalm 16:11(KJV)

"Thou art worthy, O Lord, to receive glory and honour and power: for thou hast created all things, & for thy pleasure they are and were created." Revelation 4:11(KJV)

"The thief comes only to steal and kill and destroy; I came that they may have life, and have it abundantly." John 10:10 (NASB)

*"The Lord is slow to anger, abounding in love and forgiving sin and rebellion. Yet He does not leave the guilty unpunished; He punishes the children for the sin of the fathers to the **third and fourth generation**."* Numbers 14:18 (NIV, emphasis mine)

*"...but showing love to a **thousand generations** of those who love Me and <u>keep My commandments</u>."*
Deuteronomy 5:10 (NIV, emphasis mine)

"Jesus answered, 'It was not that this man or his parents sinned, but he was born blind in order that the workings of God should be manifested (displayed and illustrated) in him." John 9:3 (AMP)

"Therefore, there is now no condemnation for those who are in Christ Jesus." Romans 8:1(NIV)

"You are living a brand new kind of life that is continually learning more and more of what is right..." Colossians 3:10 (TLB)

LESSON 2

"But Daniel resolved not to defile himself with the royal food and wine; and he asked the chief official for "... Ashpenaz ... brought into the king's service some of the Israelites from the royal family and the <u>nobility</u>." Daniel 1:3 (NIV, paraphrase mine)

He was *"well informed..."* and
"...qualified to serve in the King's palace." Daniel 1:4 (NIV)

*"Among these were some from Judah:
Daniel, Hananiah, Mishael and Azariah."*
(Referring to Shadrach, Meshach, Abednego) Daniel 1:6 (NIV)

"But Daniel resolved not to defile himself with the royal food and wine; and he asked the chief official for permission not to defile himself this way . . . Please test your servants for ten days: Give us nothing but vegetables to eat and water to drink. Then compare our appearance with that of the young men who eat the royal food, and treat your servants in accordance with what you see."
Daniel 1:8, 12, 13 (NIV)

This wasn't something new to Daniel as evidenced by his description in verse four:

He was *"without any physical defect, handsome, showing aptitude for every kind of learning, and quick to understand."*
Daniel 1: 15 (NIV)

The Result?

Of the Biblical Daniel, it was said that he *"looked better and more robust,"* had *"skill and knowledge in both books and life,"* was *"gifted in understanding,"* was *"found far superior,"* and *"ten times better"* than those who were not following the Creator's design. Daniel 1:17 (NIV)

The beginning of wisdom is this: Get wisdom.
Though it cost all you have, get understanding.
Proverbs 4:7 (NIV)

"Then God said, 'I give you every seed-bearing plant on the face of the whole earth and every tree that has fruit with seed in it. They will be yours for food. And to all the beasts of the earth and all the birds of the air and all the creatures that move on the ground—everything that has the breath of life in it—I give every green plant for food.' And it was so. God saw all that he had made, and it was very good."
Genesis 1:29-31 (NIV)

"My people are DESTROYED for lack of knowledge."
Hosea 4:6 (KJV)

"What? Know ye not that your body is the temple of the Holy Spirit? And ye are not your own, for ye are bought with a price. Therefore, GLORIFY GOD WITH YOUR BODY."
I Corinthians 6:19, 20 (KJV)

"'Everything is permissible for me' - but not everything is beneficial. 'Everything is permissible for me' - but I will not be mastered by anything." I Corinthians 6:12 (NIV)

"Give me understanding and I will keep your law and obey it with all my heart." Psalm 119:34 (NIV)

LESSON 3

"It is BETTER to spend your time at funerals than festivals for you ARE going to die, and it is a GOOD thing to think about while there is still time. Sorrow is BETTER than laughter, for sadness has a refining influence on us. Yes, a wise man thinks much of death, while the fool thinks only of having a good time now."
Ecclesiastes 7:2-4 (TLB)

*"Woe to those who call **good** bad, and **bad** good..."*
Isaiah 5:20 (personal paraphrase)

*"You made my body, Lord;
now give me sense to heed Your laws."*
Psalms 119:73 (The Living Bible)

*"Your laws are always fair,
help me to understand them and I shall live."*
Psalm 119:144 (TLB)

"There is a way that seemeth right unto a man, but the end thereof are the ways of death." Proverbs 14:12 (KJV)

"The thief comes only to steal and kill and destroy; I have come that they may have life, and have it to the full." John 10:10 (NIV)

*"Give me understanding and I will obey your instructions;
I will put them into practice with all my heart."*
Psalm 119:34 (NLV)

"As His anointing teaches you about all things...remain in Him."
1 John 2:27 (NIV)

LESSON 4

"Do not be deceived, God cannot be mocked. A man reaps what he sows." Galatians 6:7 (NIV)

"For the wrath of man worketh not the righteousness of God"
James 1:20 (KJV)

"All things are lawful for me, but not all things are profitable. All things are lawful for me, but I will not be mastered by anything." 1 Corinthians 6:12 (NASB)

LESSON 5

Jesus said, *"I know where I've come from and where I go next, You don't know where I'm from or where I'm headed."*
John 8:13-16 (MSG)

"From everyone who has been given much, much will be required" Luke 12:48, (NASB)

"Make a careful exploration of who you are and what you have been given, and then sink yourself into that. Don't be impressed with yourself. Don't compare yourself with others. Each of you must take responsibility for doing the creative best you can with your own life."
Galatians 6:4-5 (MSG)

"... so our body would not be divided. God wanted the different parts to care the same for each other. If one part of the body suffers, all the other parts suffer with it. Or if one part of our body is honored, all the other parts share its honor."
1 Corinthians 12:25-26 (NCV)

Ten times better!

LESSON 6

*"... there were 200 leaders...with their relatives...
all men who understood the temper of the times
and new the BEST COURSE...to take."*
I Chronicles 12:32 (TLB)

"[Not in your own strength] for it is God Who is all the while effectually at work in you [energizing and creating in you the power and desire], both to will and to work for His good pleasure and satisfaction and delight." Philippians 2:13 (AMP)

Scripture References

- Genesis 1:1 (NIV)
- Genesis 1:27 (NIV)
- Genesis 1:29-31 (NIV)
- Numbers 14:18 (NIV)
- Deuteronomy 5:10 (NIV)
- Deuteronomy 6:5-9 (NIV)
- Joshua 1:8 (KJV)
- I Chronicles 12:32 (TLB)
- Psalm 16:11 (KJV)
- Psalm 119:34 (NLT)
- Psalms 119:73 (TLB)
- Psalm 119:144 (TLB)
- Proverbs 4:7 (NIV)
- Proverbs 14:12 (KJV)
- Ecclesiastes 7:2-4 (TLB)
- Isaiah 5:20 (Personal Paraphrase)
- Jeremiah 29:11 (NIV)
- Daniel 1:3,4,6,8,12,13 (NIV, NLT, NIV)
- Hosea 4:6 (KJV)
- Luke 12:48 (NASB)
- John 8:13-16 (MSG)
- John 9:3 (AMP)
- John 10:10 (NIV)
- Acts 10 (MSG)
- Romans 8:1 (NIV)
- Romans 12:1, 2 (NIV)
- I Corinthians 6:12 (NASB)
- I Corinthians 6:19, 20 (KJV)
- I Corinthians 12:25-26 (NCV)
- Galatians 6:4,5 (MSG)
- Galatians 6:7 (NIV)
- Philippians 2:13 (AMP)
- Colossians 3:10 (TLB)
- 2 Timothy 3:16 (CJB)
- James 1:20 (KJV)
- 1 John 2:27 (NIV)
- Revelation 4:11 (KJV)

APPENDIX 15

Paradigm Shifts

1. INTRODUCTION (page xxxv) and again in LESSON ONE Symptoms are our friends (not the enemy) and reveal what nutrients we are low in and therefore what foods need to be added to our diet (page 3). We must build health rather than juggle symptoms (page 7).
2. LESSON ONE Life is a journey. Sometimes we get blown off course (page 9). There's no shame in that. Just adjust course. (The issue of food is about **abundant living** *not salvation*.)
3. LESSON TWO Foods are nutrient dense or nutrient robbing (page 20). Simple foods in their natural state provide all that is needed to digest and assimilate them for use in the body. Processed foods are missing key elements and thus rob the body rather than fuel it. View food as your best medicine (page 21).
4. LESSON THREE If it feels good do it and if it doesn't, don't. Definitions of "good" and "bad" (page 33). We must eat primarily for fuel and healing rather than fun, comfort and socialization (Page 35). We must work with our design, not against it. As our bodies cleanse and gain an alkaline balance, our tastes change, increasing the likelihood that we will love the foods that build our health (Page 45). Since we can acquire a taste for things that rob our health, we can also acquire a taste for those that build it. Don't let short-term pleasures rob long-term goals.
5. LESSON FOUR Use a positive approach of "adding to" rather than "taking away" (Page 55). Taking a positive approach of "yes-yes, I *get* to have all these things I have been missing out on" will cause you to crowd out (with good food) what is harming you, and you will find that your body craves the nutrient-packed foods more than nutrient-draining foods.

6. LESSON FIVE Health is holistic, and contains many elements, some of which are food, exercise, sunshine, fresh air, a non-toxic environment, meaningful relationships [spiritual and human], satisfying work, good communication and conflict resolution skills, etc. (pages 72, 80) Each of us is like a puzzle piece. We have *strengths* [something to give], *growth areas* [our road to maturity in our strengths], and *gaps* [areas where we have nothing to give; areas that need to be filled by healthy relationships] (page 76).
7. LESSON SIX The Daniel Fast is actually a Daniel FEAST and cooperates with your Creator's design for living vibrantly and abundantly (page 90).

Connect the Dots Statements

1. INTRODUCTION (page xxxv) **Connect the dots** between *how . you . feel . and . your . lifestyle*; (for the purposes of this study) primarily your food intake.

    [FEELING GOOD = LIFESTYLE]

2. LESSON ONE (page 9, 10) Are our choices taking us to illness, injury, loneliness, loss, etc. or abundant living? Where are your choices taking you?

    [CHOICE = HEADED UP Or DOWN]

3. LESSON THREE *As . our . bodies . cleanse, we . will . acquire . a . taste . for . these . foods* because they are the Creator's design. The other foods are non-foods and a lie of the evil one to cut our lives short (page 27, 36).

    [ACQUIRING A TASTE = CLEANSING & UNDERSTANDING THE BENEFITS]

Connect the dots between the *things . that . bring . us . harm . and . the . things . that . bring . us . life . in . the . long . run*! We must think about the bigger picture and how our actions affect others, our service to our Heavenly Father, and our part in history. We must tell our minds to grow up and do what is in the best interest of our bodies and our responsibilities (page 36).

[RESPONSIBLE ADULT = THINKING LONG-TERM BIG PICTURE]

Connect the dots between your *household . budget . health care . costs. and . the . concept . of . food . as . your . best . medicine* (page 49).

[FINANCES = HOUSEHOLD BUDGET; not just food budget]

4. LESSON FOUR (pages 51) Hopefully you have begun to **connect the dots** resulting in adjustments to your own life – whether in restructuring finances (homework assignment for Lesson 3) or beginning to consume living foods (homework assignment for this week's lesson). Have you noticed *an . increased . desire . to . build . a . healthy . lifestyle . and . to . be . around . people . who . desire . the . same*?

[FINANCES and RELATIONSHIPS = (need) HEALTHY SUPPORT]

LESSON FOUR (page 54) Remember that what you don't know can hurt you! Symptoms are not the enemy; they are your friends to help you know which foods (nutrients) are missing from your diet. Remember that processed foods cannot give life, and rob the body of stored nutrients which causes symptoms. Therefore, we simply must **connect the dots** between *what . we . eat . and . our . symptoms*, as well as eating *good . food . to . reverse . damage . done . by . poor . diet*.

[SYMPTOMS = FOOD]

LESSON FOUR (page 63) Great job! You have begun *a . health-building journey* that will **connect the dots** *for . a . healthy . future*, not just for you but also for your family and generations to come.

[HEALTHY BUILDING = A POSITIVE LEGACY]

5. LESSON FIVE (page 68/74) **Connect the dots** between your *food, mood, health/disease, relationships/divorce, poverty, violence, crime.*

[HEALTHY = SAFETY]

LESSON FIVE (page 77) **Connect the dots** between *your . Creator . and . yourself . as . the . created . and . His . plan . for . health.* When we are dealing with illnesses our focus must change from helping others and making contributions to society to merely surviving (page 68).

[ABUNDANT LIVING = CONNECTION WITH THE CREATOR]

6. LESSON SIX (page 78) There really *is* a way to make this journey filled with fun ... that lasts! In this final lesson together, we wrap up our **connect the dots**. We will learn 1) *how . we . get . from . where . we . are . to . where . we . want . to . be . (or need to be)*; 2) how we can transition from *filling . our . bodies . with . nutrient- robbing . foods . to . nutrient- dense . foods;* 3) how all these *changes . can . be . made . without . feeling . like . we . are . missing . out.* More than that, how it can be done in a way that 4) *everyone . on . the . journey . really . enjoys . the . "ride"*!

[DANIEL CHALLENGE = FUN - THAT <u>LASTS</u>]

READER'S DIGEST VERSION

1. Accept God as your CREATOR and seek to understand the design with which He created you.
2. Understand that SYMPTOMS ARE OUR FRIENDS who are attempting to keep us healthy and alive. They tell us how we, or our ancestor's, have violated the Creator's design and what is needed to get back on course.
3. DEFINE GOOD AND BAD according to LONG-TERM BENEFITS/DETRIMENTS rather than immediate gratification. THINK IN A BIG PICTURE of community. How does the health of the community affect the safety of the community? Being healthy is fun that lasts!
4. Take the necessary steps to ACQUIRE A TASTE for that which brings lasting benefit
5. Learn the difference between NUTRIENT DENSE and NUTRIENT ROBBING foods
6. Understand that health is about a LIFESTYLE, not a diet, and adjustments need to be made to get back on course in all areas of life
7. Remove condemnation and shame by reframing LIFE AS A JOURNEY in which we learn through antonyms as well as synonyms i.e. perfectionism is not welcome. DISCOVERING TRUTH THROUGH THE CONSEQUENCES OF OUR CHOICES IS A GREAT WAY TO LEARN. Then, ASK GOD FOR EMPOWERMENT to walk in that truth.
8. Focus on ADDING TO, NOT TAKING AWAY. The Daniel Fasts of today are actually Daniel *FEASTS!*
9. Fly in a V; connect with those who are ready to focus on building health beginning with one's biological family, church family, neighbors, workplace, children's friends, etc. (you get the picture) i.e. ESTABLISH A STRONG SUPPORT SYSTEM.
10. To finance the lifestyle change; one must focus on a household budget not the food budget. ONE COST ELIMINATES ANOTHER. FOOD IS YOUR BEST MEDICINE.

APPENDIX 16

Talking to Your Health Care Provider

Before making significant changes to their lifestyle, we encourage our clients to inform their health care provider of their intent to make significant, health-building, lifestyle adjustments, etc. The conversation might proceed like the following:

"I am not here with any particular symptom or complaint today, doctor. I just wanted to inform you that I have been learning the benefits of assuming responsibility for building my physical and relational health with natural means. It is my understanding that, as I adopt this new lifestyle, my body will become more alkaline (rather than acid) and the possibility of my symptoms going away increase greatly. There are no promises, but this has the potential of eliminating my need for medication. Would you be willing to monitor my progress and lower my medication amounts as appropriate?"

If the doctor is uncooperative, you have the right to seek a second opinion and "hire" a doctor who will help you with your health-building goals.

Another option would be to add a Naturopathic Doctor (N.D.) or a chiropractor (D.C.) to your health building team.

TOPICAL INDEX BY CHAPTER

Introduction:

xxv	DHS Meth Home Investigation
xxvii	Dan Buettner, National Geographic, Blue Zones, Dr. Oz, Loma Linda, CA, Marg Jetton
xxviii	Standard American Diet (S.A.D.)
xxxii	Common vs. Normal
xxxiv	Dying too long and living too short
xxxiv	Quality of life AND quantity of life
xxxiv	Betsy's own 100 day transformation with nutrient dense foods
xxxv	How this book can help

Lesson One REALITY (Experiments, Experiences and Statistics):

1	Personal Story: Car Overheating on Family Outing
2	Paradigm shift: Symptoms - friend(s) rather than the enemy
2	Warning lights on your car
4	*Dead Doctors Don't Lie*
4	Juggling Symptoms or Building Health
4	Pottinger Experiment
5	Horticulture and Show Animals
5	Senior Care Experiences
6	Granny Dumping
7	Senior Years Options
7	Common vs. Normal
8	Holistic approach - spiritual component of knowing God as Creator (not just Father and Savior)
8	Generational Curses and Blessings
9	Paradigm Shift: Ship's trip New York to London/No Condemnation
9	Connect the Dots: Long run/short run decision-making
10	How our choices affect others

Empower Your Purpose: The Daniel FEAST!

Lesson Two UNDERSTANDING (How It Happened – Blown Off Course):

12	Personal Story: Juicing, roundup, gardening, parental heroes
13	Historic Role Model: DANIEL
14	Dr. Lorraine Day
16	Wool sweater illustration
17	Meet your Creator and His "Owner's Manual"
18	Real Food vs. Junk Food
18, 22	Adrenal burnout
19	Drinking with meals
19	Processed foods
19	Overheating
19	Oxidation
20	Paradigm Shift: nutrient packed/nutrient rich vs nutrient robbing
21	Toxins - embalming
21	Body Fuel vs. Car Fuel
22	Stimulation vs. Fuel
22	Car and the 18 wheeler truck
22	Salvation issue or abundant living issue
23	Right foods prepared the wrong way
23	Hierarchy of Food Preparation

Lesson Three SHIFTING (More Paradigms for Transitioning Back on Course):

26	Personal Story: Living in the barn, smoking, chewing tobacco, carbonated beverages
27, 36	Connect the Dots: Acquire a taste
28-33	Nutrient Dense and Transitional Food Options
31	Paul Zane Piltzer "The Dairy Deception"
31	Soy bean products
31, 32	Vegetarian/vegan protein sources

33	Paradigm Shift: From "If it feels good do it, and if it doesn't don't!" to "If it's good for me, do it and grow to appreciate it (and maybe even love it!)"
33	Paradigm Shift: Definitions of "Good" and "Bad"
35	Paradigm Shift: In order to gain health, one must eat primarily for fuel and healing rather than temporary comfort and socializing
35, 36	Acquire a Taste
37	Cleansing and taste changes
38	Energy Economics
40	Digestion Time Table
41	The "Daylight Diet"
42	The Daniel FEAST (5 key questions)
42	5 Key Words
44	Signature Drink
44	Paradigm Shift: Acid alkaline and taste change
44	ANDI Scale
46	Barley Max from HAcres
47	Daily Schedule
48	Drinking in between meals

Lesson Four HOW-TOS (The Set Up and the Process for the Daniel FEAST):

50	Personal Story: Buford Family and My Sons
51	Establishing your support system – 5 tips to getting your family on board
53	Personal Story: Building family health even when struggling as a single parent
55	Paradigm Shift: Positive approach
55	"Adding To" not "Taking Away"
55	Crowd out the harmful foods with the good foods
56	Your tastes will change
56	"Cold turkey" or "start slow and work into it" approach
57	Setting up your Kitchen for Good Food Fast
59	Shopping

60	Teamwork and Your Support System
61	Preparing the Produce for "Good Food Fast"
62	Arranging your refrigerator

Lesson Five SYNERGY (Your Lifestyle on Course with Your Creator, Family & Friends):

65	Personal Story: Fish fry, egg roles, pizza, church and local families
66	Flying in a "V"
67	Elephant herd - Need each other in the Spiritual Battle
67	Rugged American Individualism
67	Not designed to do life alone
68	Crumbling Families Statistics
69	How Our Lifestyle Affects Our Responsibilities
69	Homemaking Role
70	Scriptures validating roles
70	How Our Lifestyle Affects Our Relationships
71	Mood Affects Relationships
72	Miracle in Wisconsin
72	Relationships Affect societal safety, peace and happiness
72	Ten Unchangeables
72	Areas to Define Identity
73	Listing of Identity Resources
74	Importance of Family of Origin
75	Choosing a Life Partner and Additional Business/Ministry Teams
76	Terms for Positive Identity (strengths, growth areas, gaps)

Lesson Six GAME-ON (Four Levels of the DANIEL CHALLENGE):

78	Personal Story: Housework with five sons made fun
78	Connecting the Dots
79	Growth Analysis
80	Lifestyle rather than Diet
81	Nutritional Analysis; the emotional, relational, and

Ten times better!

	physical connection
83	Replacement Recipe Sources
83	Readiness Assessment Questions
85	Customizing Your Plan
86	The DANIEL CHALLENGES
88	Suggestions to those who are DANIEL FASTING
89	Score Cards for The DANIEL CHALLENGES
90	The Empowered Focus

APPENDIX 1:   Statistics
APPENDIX 2:   Connecting Your Dots (Identify YOUR Symptoms)
APPENDIX 3:   How Food & Family Have Changed Over Time
APPENDIX 4:   Family Systems Evaluation
APPENDIX 5:   Peter's Vision (Scriptures)
APPENDIX 6:   DANIEL CHALLENGE Replacement Plan & Journal
APPENDIX 7:   Budget Worksheet
APPENDIX 8:   Cravings
APPENDIX 9:   Guide to Soaking Nuts and Seeds
APPENDIX 10:   Additional Tips for Finicky or Reluctant Eaters
APPENDIX 11:   The Dirty Dozen and Clean Fifteen of Produce
APPENDIX 12:   Miracle in Wisconsin
APPENDIX 13:   Prayers for Being Born Again & God's Help as Your Creator
APPENDIX 14:   Scriptures for Reference and Memorization
APPENDIX 15:   Paradigm Shifts and Connect the Dots Statements
APPENDIX 16:   Talking to Your Health Care Provider

FOR SMALL GROUP DISCUSSION

LESSON 1

Discussion Questions:

1. What stats in Appendix 1 stood out most to you?
2. Discuss the three lifestyles that were revealed in the Introduction. Which lifestyle do you associate with you and your family? What is lacking – knowledge, understanding, support, a plan – that keeps you from making positive lifestyle choices?
3. What are your feelings about the paradigm shift concerning *symptoms*: (a) as something to stop immediately and at all costs, or (b) as gifts from God to help us know what lifestyle adjustments we need to make?
4. What would motivate a person in the illegal drug lifestyle to want to change?
5. What would motivate a person in the typical American lifestyle to want to change?
6. Have you noticed, like Dr. Pottinger, the deterioration of our generation's health? How does this relate to the change in food (Appendix 2)?
7. Honestly evaluate your life. Have you been focused on building health or juggling symptoms? What is the difference?

8. Have you felt condemning pressure from society or other teachings/programs in regard to making changes in your physical and relational health? Has that been effective?
9. How do you feel about this "guilt-free" approach to get society back on course by being part of a transitional generation?
10. Discuss the scriptures covered in this lesson. For your convenience, all scriptures and their references are listed in Appendix 14.

LESSON 2

Discussion Questions:

1. Describe a "holistic approach" to life.
2. When Dr. Lorraine Day was diagnosed with cancer, what changes did she make? Why was this enough or not enough?
3. Discuss Daniel's four main beliefs. Do you feel these are important for <u>you</u> to believe as well?
4. Discuss the results of DANIEL'S 10-day test in history as compared to Loma Linda's The Blue Zone's results. Is Biblical history ringing true through the ages? Do you see the value of joining the company of Daniel and those who are following his lifestyle?
5. Who decides what humans should eat? Why is it vital to follow the Manufacturer's plan?
6. What is the difference between **real** food and **junk** food?
7. What happens when foods are processed?
8. What is causing so many Americans to experience adrenal burnout?
9. Discuss the suggested scriptures.
10. Discuss the difference between "salvation through the blood of Jesus Christ" and "abundant living by applying the principles from the Creator's guidebook".

LESSON 3

Discussion Questions:

1. Describe "transitional foods".
2. Discuss the paradigm shifts listed in this chapter.
3. What were the definitions of "good" and "bad"? Were they surprising? What did you learn about the truth regarding these words as they pertain to food?
4. Does "Acquiring a Taste" make sense? How will you apply this concept? (Remember the three steps given.)
5. Our culture is so big on eating a "good breakfast". Discuss the digestion timetable as it pertains to early morning academic or mental business demands in early morning. How long does it take for typical breakfast foods to actually be available for energy for the body? Thus, if we need energy at 8:00 a.m., when could that fuel absorb into the body? If unable to do it then, what foods could we eat to provide the energy needed, when it's needed? Can our breakfast actually *hinder* our productivity if consumed: (1) in the wrong time; (2) in the wrong amount; or (3) in nutrient robbing foods?
6. Discuss the digestion time frames as they pertain to a good night's rest, or an athlete playing in a tournament.
7. The average American spends 91 cents out of every dollar on processed foods. As one works to change that, what are the five key words to remember? Share with the group some of the *living foods* you are adding to your diet.
8. Did anyone try juicing? If so, what combination of vegetables and fruit did you like best?
9. In Appendix 8, you learned how to deal with cravings you may experience as you transition to the *Daniel Lifestyle*. What are some of the questions you need to ask when you crave things you know are counter productive to building health? Did anyone try this technique this week? If so, did you find

yourself giving in to the craving or choosing a healthy alternative?
10. Did you review the DANIEL CHALLENGE REPLACEMENT PLAN? Share with the group some replacements you have already made.
11. As a group, quote the *Scripture to Remember*.

LESSON 4

Discussion Questions:

1. What is your biggest concern about adopting a health-building lifestyle?
2. Which is more economical – paying for good nutrition or paying for health care, medications, surgeries, etc.?
3. What level of support do you see developing among your family and friends? (Review the five keys to getting your family on board.)
4. What new foods did you try this week? Did you get your family involved? Did you make changes to your shopping methods and your food preparation? Did you find our suggestions for these helpful?
5. Discuss the Scriptures found in the lesson.

LESSON 5

Discussion Questions:

1. Discuss the birds flying in a "V". Why is this important? How does it apply to you? Review Ephesians 6:12 and John 10:10.
2. In what ways have you noticed food affecting your relationships and ability to function well?

3. Is there a correlation between health of the family, marital satisfaction, the divorce rate, the anger of today's youth and our lifestyles, roles, diet...?
4. How does healthy food affect the family differently than a family who ingests only those things considered "poor food choices"? Discuss the role of nutrition in deviant behavior...your own as well as society's violence and crime.
5. Take some time to share who you are (remember the "Ten Unchangeables"?), where you are going, and with whom you are going. Rejoice in the way God made you, the gifts He has given you, the family He has blessed you with, and the path He has chosen for your life!
6. Review the scriptures covered in this lesson.

LESSON 6

Discussion Questions:

1. Share some things you have added to your diet and lifestyle since your journey began with *Daniel & Company*. How have these affected you – physically, emotionally and relationally?
2. How have you found that food has an emotional and relational connection? What foods do you think of when you think of family gatherings or celebrations? How can you incorporate *living* foods to these special times?
3. What do you see as the <u>most difficult</u> part of this adjustment period? What do you see as the <u>easiest</u> part?
4. Did you find any new recipes this week that you would like to share?
5. What are your personal goals?
6. What can you do to make this journey more do-able and fun? Are you ready? Then ... GAME ON!!!!!

AUTHOR'S PAGE

The majority of the principles shared in this book, *Empower Your Purpose: The Daniel FEAST*, were gathered and applied during Betsy's 10 year single parenting season. As a young mother she found herself in poverty, yet with responsibility to help five young sons to adulthood. She knew that if she were ill, she couldn't *fulfill her purpose* as their mother. She simply HAD to have energy and clear thinking, a positive attitude and be disease free. Her sons were depending on her.

Today, Betsy and all five sons are healthy and thriving. Each of her sons are married, gainfully employed, own their own homes, pay their taxes, make volunteer contributions into society, have a strong tradition of faith, love and respect one another. Among this family, they have more than twenty degrees completed or in the process. They enjoy the presence of matriarch/patriarchs from The Great Generation. Their family is continually enjoying the growing number of vibrant, delightful grand children, with numbers thirteen and fourteen having been born this year.

Although, she wouldn't consider herself a foodie, Betsy (as a certified raw chef) thoroughly enjoys preparing health-building foods for those she loves; chatting about health and life all the while. Betsy is one who enjoys the dream, but she is equally characterized as one who does the work it takes to make the vision a reality. She continually dreams and plans, implements, learns, grows, dreams and plans some more. Betsy relishes her faith, family, friends, food, books, bicycling, swimming, jogging, step aerobics, and is a life-long-learner.

Betsy and her husband, John, live in a condominium in downtown Tulsa. John has served as a minister for over 45 years and is currently employed as a Hospice Chaplain. Together they are certified with Dr. George Malkmus as two of over 10,000 Health Ministers. They have created a social service with a strong focus on the physical and relational health of the single parent household and foster children. Betsy also enjoys mediating for Oklahoma Supreme Court in Family/Divorce and Child Welfare cases. Watch for her next book *From Welfare to Wealth Through Wellness* and additional services that will enhance the application of these life-changing truths on her blog http://www.makingthyme.com/betsy-s-blog.html.

To contact Betsy for consulting and/or speaking please email:

betsy@MAKINGthyme.com

SPECIAL NOTE

Made in the USA
Middletown, DE
21 March 2015